Insights 1

A Content-based Approach to Academic Preparation

Linda Jensen
University of California, Los Angeles

Lyn Repath-Martos
University of California, Los Angeles

Jan Frodesen
University of California, Santa Barbara

Christine Holten
University of California, Los Angeles

Donna Brinton, Project Coordinator
University of California, Los Angeles

Longman

Insights 1: A Content-based Approach to Academic Preparation

Pearson Education, 10 Bank St., White Plains, N.Y. 10606

Editorial Director: Joanne Dresner
Senior Acquisitions Editor: Allen Ascher
Development Editor: Kathleen M. Smith
Production Editor: Liza Pleva
Text design: Christine Gehring Wolf
Cover design: Pinho Graphics
Composition: Publication Services
Photo and text credits appear on pages 189–191.

Library of Congress Cataloging-in-Publication Data

Jensen, Linda, [Date.]
    Insights I : a content-based ESL text for academic preparation /
Linda Jensen . . . [et. al] ; Donna Brinton, project coordinator.
        p.   cm.
    ISBN 0-201-89854-3
    1. English language—Textbooks for foreign speakers. 2. English
language—Composition and exercises. I. Brinton, Donna.
II. Title.
PE1128.J48   1997
428.2'4--dc21   96-46288
                                                               CIP

12 13 14 15   CRS   12 11 10

Dedication

We dedicate this book to the content area professors who renewed our faith in the possibility of excellent university teaching: Donald Cosentino (Folklore), Jeffrey Lew (Atmospheric Sciences), John Laslett (History), and Nancy Levine (Anthropology).

Contents

Acknowledgments

This project was envisioned and conceived under the close scrutiny of Joanne Dresner, Editorial Director at Addison Wesley Longman. It was nurtured throughout its process by Allen Ascher, Senior Acquisitions Editor, and had all its rough edges smoothed over by Kathy Smith, formerly of Addison Wesley Longman, who saw us through the development stage, spending hours of her time editing our prose and gently suggesting changes that greatly improved the pedagogical quality of the finished product. Finally, it was polished in the production stages by Liza Pleva. Under Liza's supervision, the manuscript took shape and began to resemble a real book rather than a collection of manuscript pages. Additional help was provided by Amy Durfy, Senior Administrative Assistant, and by Polli Heyden, who helped with permissions. To all the above individuals, we express our extreme appreciation and admiration for their professionalism.

Perhaps more than to anyone else, we are indebted to Drs. Donald Cosentino, Jeffrey Lew, John Laslett, and Nancy Levine for so kindly allowing us to invade their classrooms, tape their lectures, borrow their reference materials, and use their course readings and assignments as the cornerstones of this project. Without their support, consent, and enthusiasm for our project, this book would not exist.

For their indispensible services (such as videotaping and editing, tape transcription, library runs, artwork, photocopying, proofreading, editing, etc.), we are truly indebted to the following work study assistants in the UCLA Department of TESL & Applied Linguistics: Joseph Choi, Zalika Davis, Eric Franklin, Rahel Getachew, Beth Gregory, Jerry Ching-Jen Huang, James Jauregui, Edward Kim, Clinton Lee, Greg Lyon, Margarita Mkrtchyan, Elysabeth Nguyen, Nicholas Nguyen, Susan Reese, Ruth Rivera, Soo Bin Shin, James Suh, Jimmy Trinh, Mike Wang, Ha Cuc Emma Truong, Vu-Uyen Nguyen, Sasha Mosely, Kevin Tucker, Veronica Peet, Anna McKay, Julie Lin, Amy Barranco, Eunice Quezon, Vy Nguyen, Catherine Trinidad, Shannon Cisch, Maura Newberry, Darius Degher, Fumitaka Hayashi, Joy Jacob, and Sung Park.

We are also grateful to those who piloted our materials or otherwise gave us feedback: Janet Goodwin, Bob Agajeenian, and Gaby Solomon at UCLA and Randy Rightmire, Janet Kayfetz, and Jill Snyder at UCSB. These individuals pointed out many problems in the manuscript that we had overlooked in our initial development of the materials and served as the inspiration for numerous activities that were incorporated into the final product. Needless to say, any remaining flaws are due to oversights or shortcomings on our part.

We express our sincere gratitude to our families and friends for their patience and support; additional thanks are due to Sandy Wallace and Mila August at UCLA for providing administrative assistance and for tolerating the chaos that often ensued as we scrambled to meet deadlines. Finally, we wish to thank Drs. Marianne Celce-Murcia and Dorothy Danielson for being our mentors and encouraging us to reach our full professional potential.

Introduction

OVERVIEW

Insights 1 is designed to equip ESL students to cope with the English language demands of academia. The text is focused primarily on the academic skills of reading, writing, listening, and speaking, with an emphasis on writing. We have integrated these skills with short grammar lessons, all in a content-based approach. A basic premise of the text is that, in order to effectively approach any college writing task, students must be prepared to synthesize material from multiple authentic sources, gleaning information from lectures and written and visual sources. For the best result, students must use all four skills of reading, writing, listening, and speaking to produce a written assignment.

Insights 1 is targeted at matriculated ESL students, specifically, the upper end of the community college spectrum, or those students intending to transfer to a four-year university. It is also appropriate for the upper levels of intensive language programs, where students are being prepared to enter English-medium colleges and universities.

RATIONALE

Many ESL students enrolled in U.S. colleges enter higher education with a fairly high degree of general English language proficiency. Studies have shown, however, that this proficiency is not sufficient for dealing with the complex demands of the university. These students must gain a proficiency in the register of academic English (Cummins, 1979; Collier, 1987). The goal of this text is to provide students with academic language skills that will enable them to succeed in their courses across the curriculum.

Much insight into English for Academic Purposes (EAP) curricular issues is provided by the body of literature that describes the academic language needs of these students (Kroll, 1979; Ostler, 1980; Johns, 1981; Bridgeman & Carlson, 1984; Horowitz, 1986; Santos, 1988; Spack, 1988; Fulwiler & Young, 1990). Among the recommendations made are the following:

1. Authentic materials and tasks gathered from across the disciplines should form the core of the EAP curriculum. Tasks should provide students with the tools for synthesizing information from multiple sources, for reading critically, and for efficiently processing academic information. Similarly, the development of learning strategies and metacognitive/metalinguistic skills should be introduced and reinforced.

2. Personal or writer-based writing, although it may lead to more reader-based texts, should not be the end goal of the academic writing curriculum. Emphasis should be placed instead on the research paper, summary writing, and analytical writing (including essay-exam writing).

3. The EAP curriculum should avoid "one-shot" assignments and instead require students to follow a more sequenced approach (involving notetaking, summarizing, journal writing, multiple drafts of writing assignments, etc.) as preliminary steps toward a more polished product.

4. Listening in an academic context requires the development of the same comprehension and critical analytical skills as those required for successful academic reading and writing.

5. Students should be encouraged to be active researchers or ethnographers of the academic discourse communities in which they are engaged

APPROACH

Insights 1 has grown out of the authors' long-term experience with matriculated ESL students and represents our effort to construct a meaningful and motivating content-based curriculum that addresses their academic language needs. Materials from various disciplines (in the form of authentic university reading assignments and lectures) form the cornerstone of the teaching materials. Each unit simulates the process that ESL students actually experience in their university courses as they attend lectures, do assigned course readings, participate in discussion, and elucidate ideas in written form (e.g., midterm exams, final exams, and term papers). Thus, each unit weaves together listening, speaking, reading, and writing about one high-interest topic from a university discipline.

The materials acknowledge the need for university students to command a high level of accuracy and fluency in their oral and written output. Therefore, grammar and vocabulary development are given an integral and integrated place. The treatment of grammar and lexicon in these materials always derives from and occurs in a rich and authentic discourse context. The materials encourage students to generate, analyze, and revise text to practice reading and writing certain discourse-governed and grammatically based structures within the context of larger discourse.

AUDIENCE AND PURPOSE

Insights 1 addresses the needs of the upper-level community college student or the entering four-year college student. These students need a combination of oral language opportunities and attention to English literacy. Thus the text emphasizes the oral/aural skills that allow students preliminary access to content material and establish a foundation for further academic language development. The units consist of videotaped lecture segments, accompanying academic readings, and related literary passages. In the related language and writing tasks, the focus is on schema building for listening and reading comprehension purposes, skill building, and development of vocabulary and grammar skills needed to comprehend, discuss, and write about the unit content. Writing tasks begin by probing students' personal reactions in the form of journal entries about key issues from the content readings and lectures. The lectures and reading passages require students to apply cognitive processing strategies and exercise advanced language skills.

UNIT ORGANIZATION

1. *Insights 1* consists of four units drawn from the humanities, the physical sciences, and the social sciences. These discipline-specific units are further subdivided into three chapters, each of which treats the same high-interest topic from the discipline from a variety of perspectives.

2. Each of the four units contains three chapters: Introduction, Exploration, and Expansion.

   - *Introduction*   The first chapter of the unit serves as a general introduction to the topic to be explored. The readings and lecture segments are accessible to those with little or no prior knowledge of the topic, and they aim to generate interest and enhance understanding of the issues.

   - *Exploration*   The second chapter of each unit introduces students to the primary academic source materials (i.e., academic readings and lectures). The related tasks promote critical understanding and require students to synthesize material from a variety of sources.

   - *Expansion*   In the third chapter of each unit, the readings and lectures take a larger view of the academic concepts. Tasks in this chapter require students to connect the knowledge gained from the previous chapters to human life and concerns as represented in the literature readings. The final writing assignment requires students to synthesize and evaluate the issues of the unit and to present their point of view in an academic essay.

3. All lecture segments are authentic and were videotaped in actual university classes. The videotaped materials are supplemented by the authentic reading materials assigned for

this course and other topically related readings (including literature). Many of the unit's tasks replicate those used in the actual content classes.

4. Special features contained in *Insights 1* include Academic Strategies, Targeting Vocabulary, and Targeting Grammar. These features, located throughout the chapters, help students expand their range of metacognitive strategies, enlarge their general academic and field-specific vocabulary, edit for common language errors, and employ more sophisticated grammatical structures in their oral and written output. All issues pertaining to language are systematically addressed from a discourse perspective.

5. The chapters contain multiple "writing to learn" opportunities, including journal and reading-response assignments and in-class writing assignments. All writing tasks in the units take a process approach and are set up so that students have multiple opportunities to draft and polish their ideas and language.

CHAPTER ORGANIZATION

The three thematically interwoven chapters contained in each discipline-specific unit are further subdivided into the following sections: Exploring the Concepts, Working with Sources, and Integrating Perspectives.

1. ***Exploring the Concepts***   This section encourages students to apply their background knowledge as they approach the new concepts and, therefore, promotes interest in the content. The activities provide a foundation for the academic material that follows in Working with Sources. Subsections that may be included are

   - *Exploring through Visual Images*   Visuals from everyday life (e.g., drawings, photographs, cartoons) activate the students' understanding of the content to which they will be exposed.

   - *Exploring Background Knowledge*   Students' prior knowledge about the topic is tapped through a variety of activities such as brainstorming and values clarification.

   - *Exploring through Writing*   Students are encouraged to share personal experiences or reactions via a journal entry related to the topic.

   - *Exploring through Discussion*   Students share personal experiences and opinions and apply concepts to real-life situations.

2. ***Working with Sources***   Students encounter introductory or core readings and videotaped lecture segments that present the basic issues or concepts. Subsections that may be included are

   - *Understanding through Visual Images*   Visuals such as photos, charts, and graphs from popular sources and academic textbooks allow students to preview the issues contained in the listening and reading tasks that follow.

   - *Understanding through Listening*   The lecture segment expands students' information about the academic content. Graphic organizers are utilized to aid students in recognizing the important ideas and the structure of the lecture. The related tasks encourage critical analysis, guiding students in their notetaking and listening comprehension.

   - *Understanding through Reading*   The reading presents students with information that either is directly linked to the listening or expands on the topic. Students are guided toward a fuller understanding of the text through tasks that encourage text processing.

   - *Understanding through Literature*   A literature excerpt or short piece that relates to the academic reading and listening segments allows students to explore the topic from a literary perspective, fostering critical application of the unit's issues.

3. ***Integrating Perspectives*** In this section the concept or issue is examined in greater depth, either by offering an additional perspective or by asking students to apply the concepts learned to a new situation. Students demonstrate their understanding by applying, analyzing, or evaluating the concepts of the unit. Subsections that may be included are

- *Applying the Concepts* This activity promotes synthesis or application of the information from Working with Sources, often through the use of graphic organizers or visuals.

- *Analyzing through Visual Images* Students react critically to visual images such as cartoons or illustrations, drawing on their understanding of the topic.

- *Analyzing through Discussion* Through discussion (e.g., ranking or problem-solving tasks), students enhance their understanding of the reading and videotaped lecture material to which they have been exposed.

- *Evaluating through Literature* Students read and react to a piece of unadapted literature (e.g., a short story, an extract from a longer work of fiction) and critically apply one of the frameworks or theories from the unit to this work.

- *Evaluating through Writing* This writing task allows students to synthesize the main ideas from the sources, employing their expanded knowledge of grammar and vocabulary. Within each unit, the writing tasks progress from personal to academic. Each unit culminates in a writing assignment for which students are provided clear guidelines and instructions to enhance their academic writing skills.

REFERENCES

Bridgeman, B., & Carlson, S. (1984). *Survey of academic writing tasks required of graduate and undergraduate foreign students.* TOEFL Research Report No. 15. Princeton, NJ: Educational Testing Service.

Collier, V. P. (1987). Age and rate of acquisition of second language for academic purposes. *TESOL Quarterly, 21,* 617–641.

Cummins, J. (1979). Linguistic interdependence and the educational development of bilingual children. *Review of Educational Research, 49*(2), 222–251.

Fulwiler, T., & Young, A. (Eds.). (1990). *Programs that work: Models and methods for writing across the curriculum.* Portsmouth, NH: Boynton/Cook Heinemann.

Horowitz, D. M. (1986). What professors actually require: Academic tasks for the ESL classroom. *TESOL Quarterly, 20*(3), 445–462.

Johns, A. M. (1981). Necessary English: A faculty survey. *TESOL Quarterly, 15*(1), 51–57.

Kroll, B. (1979). A survey of the writing needs of foreign and American college freshmen. *ELT Journal, 33*(3), 219–226.

Ostler, S. (1980). A survey of academic needs for advanced ESL. *TESOL Quarterly, 14*(4), 489–502.

Santos, T. (1988). Professors' reactions to the academic writing of nonnative-speaking students. *TESOL Quarterly, 22*(1), 69–90.

Spack, R. (1988). Initiating ESL students into the academic discourse community: How far should we go? *TESOL Quarterly, 22*(1), 29–51.

INSIGHTS FROM FOLKLORE

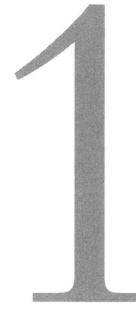

INTRODUCTION:
MATERIAL FOLK CULTURE

Folklore is traditional customs, beliefs, etc. of people, countries or regions.

All cultures find their reflection in their cultural artifacts, such as their folk tales and folk art objects. These artifacts tell us much about the people who live in the culture. This unit focuses on material folk culture, or the concrete objects that individuals make and surround themselves with. For the folklorist—the social scientist who studies material folk objects—these objects can provide valuable clues to a people's way of life, their values and beliefs, and any changes in these values and beliefs that occur over time.

Exploring the Concepts

EXPLORING THROUGH VISUAL IMAGES

TASK 1: Imagine that it is the year 3000. You are a folklorist working at the Museum of Cultural History and you've been given the task of cataloging the objects pictured here and on the next page. With a partner or in small groups, discuss where you think these objects might have come from and what meaning they had in that culture.

Targeting Vocabulary: Describing Objects

The following words and phrases are useful for describing objects. Consult a dictionary for any unfamiliar words.

SHAPE	MATERIAL	DESCRIPTIVE PHRASES
round, circular	wood, wooden	decorated with
square	metal (gold, silver, brass, etc.)	painted (with)
rectangular		carved (with)
oblong	stone, bone, shell	surrounded by
pointed	straw, raffia, reed, grass	with
oval	clay	made of
	paper	

Examples:

It's a small **reed** basket **decorated with** sea **shells.**

The mask is **made of** red **clay** and it's **painted with** black geometrical designs.

The face is **oblong** and it's **surrounded by** feathers.

The **carved wooden** horse has a **pointed** nose and long, skinny legs.

🌀 Targeting Grammar: Sequencing Adjectives

When more than one adjective is used to describe an object, the adjectives usually occur in a particular order:

1. OPINION	2. SIZE	3. SHAPE	4. AGE	5. COLOR	6. MATERIAL
beautiful	tiny	round	old	ochre	wooden
lovely	small	circular	new	black	obsidian
ugly	big	oval	contemporary	multicolored	lacquer
well-preserved	large	square	antique	blue	clay
exquisite	medium-sized	rectangular	modern	gray	straw

Examples:

It's a **small** **circular** **gold** brooch.
     (size)   (shape)   (material)

It's a **lovely** **old** **black** **lacquer** box.
    (opinion) (age) (color) (material)

It's a **well-preserved** **medium-sized** **obsidian** arrowhead.
    (opinion)   (size)   (material)

Note: It is rare for English speakers to use more than three descriptive adjectives in front of a noun.

TASK 2: Decide whether each of the following sentences contains adjectives in the preferred order. Make corrections for the sentences that do not have the appropriate word order.

1. It's a red round pottery jug with a black lovely design.

It's a round red pottery jug with a lovely black design.

2. It's a metal hexagonal box decorated with small beautiful figures.

It's a hexagonal metal box decorated with beautiful small figures.

3. It's an old terra-cotta vase complete with large, brightly painted animals and flowers.

It's an old terra-cotta vase complete with brightly, large painted animals and flowers. No change. O.K.

4. It's a brown wooden tiny carving of antique unusual instruments.

It's a tiny brown wooden carving of unusual antique instruments.

TASK 3: Using as many of the words from the list on page 3 as you can, write five more descriptions of objects.

1. _____

_____

_____

2. _____

_____

_____

3. _____

_____

_____

4. _____

_____

_____

5. _____

_____

_____

TASK 4: For the museum catalog, you have been asked to write a physical description of each object pictured in Task 1. Write the description below, paying attention to the order of adjectives in each phrase.

Object #1: _They are ugly small old dolls made of wooden._

_____

Object #2: _It's a strange large story on the stone picture. good one: It's a beautiful old stone carving depicting a wedding ceremony surrounded by soldiers._

Object #3: _It's a ugly tall god made of wooden._

_____

Object #4: _This is a beautiful tiny wooden man who has winds._

_____

EXPLORING THROUGH DISCUSSION

Folk objects kept in families can take on special or sentimental value for each new generation.

TASK 5: Read the following description of a handmade folk object. Why do you think this object fascinates the author's children? Why did the author find it difficult to throw this object away? After reading, discuss these questions with a partner.

The Children's Room

Propped in the center of the *mantel* is an old wall hanging: a wood *bas-relief* of a tavern, including kitchen, dining hall, and bedrooms. Every object and gesture is carved and painted with cunning attention: dinner plates the size of dimes, a butter churn with a three-inch *dash*, washtubs, rolling pin, crucifix, table and benches, a clock whose hands read a quarter past five, hats hanging on hooks by the door, an accordion, two flowerpots, shotgun, and stove. My grandfather, who was apprenticed in 1904 to a cabinetmaker in Berlin (he was fourteen), acquired the hanging, which was made in the Black Forest. It used to contain a working music box, and just under the *eaves* is a brass key that no longer turns. The hidden mechanism once played, my grandfather told me, a feeble *polka*.

As a child I spent many hours staring at the tavern's tiny furnishings, at once seduced and bewildered by the very nature of bas-relief, neither flat picture nor free sculpture, a doll house enduring an uneasy metamorphosis from three dimensions to two. Before we had children, I moved the tavern from closet to basement to guest room and back to closet, never knowing what to do with it until our children showed me.

"Take it down! I want to look at it up close!" one of them will say. The request is never more avid than when the children are ill, and I can remember exactly how fever enhanced the little row of frying pans hung over the stove, *gilded* the flowers painted on cupboard doors the size of my thumbnail.

Source: Kathryn Harrison (1995, October 16). *The New Yorker,* 149–150.

---

mantel – shelf above a fireplace; *bas-relief* – a two-dimensional art object in which the shapes stand out slightly from the background, which has been cut away; *dash* – the pole used to stir the butter in a butter churn; *eaves* – edges of the roof; *polka* – a German dance; *gilded* – covered with gold

TASK 6: Think of a handmade object from your childhood or one that you currently own. Describe this object and explain its significance for you to a partner. Here are some phrases that may be useful for this description:

I have an old . . .	My mother/father had an old . . .
There is/are . . .	I/we used to . . .
There was/were . . .	Unlike today's ___, it . . .
It has/had . . .	What was interesting/fascinating about it was that it had . . .

Working with Sources

UNDERSTANDING THROUGH READING

Folk objects, such as those you've looked at and read about so far, constitute material folk culture and help define a people and the times they lived in.

TASK 7: Read the two definitions of folk objects, focusing on the examples of material folk culture that both authors provide.

Definition 1

Folk objects materialize tradition. Typically learned by imitating the work of community or family members and by participating in local customs, folk objects exhibit the repetition and variation common to other forms of folklore such as tales, songs, proverbs, and riddles. Of course, folk objects show the interconnections common to all forms of folklore. A house, a carving, or a food dish reflects shared experience, community ideas, and values connecting individuals and groups to one another and to the environment. To stress these interconnections, the term "material culture" is often used to point to the weave of objects in the everyday lives of individuals and communities.

Source: Simon J. Bronner (1986). Folk objects. In E. Oring (Ed.), *Folk groups and folklore genres: An introduction* (p. 199). Logan, UT: Utah State University Press.

Definition 2

Material folk culture is probably the most difficult aspect of folklore to define. For instance, are homemade roadside signs folk art? How about a large metal fish used to advertise a seafood restaurant? How about a snowman or a scarecrow? Is a quilt made by studying a book a folk object? How about needlework drawings done by young schoolgirls in the last century that were usually made by following a preset design?

There really are few hard-and-fast rules or tests for material culture. The key word here is "traditional." This tradition must be, in Henry Glassies' words, "old and acceptable to the individual or group which produced it." In other words, there must be a tradition behind the object so that the craftsperson regards the object as old or "old-fashioned." This tradition must be part of the producer's own folk group—not part of "popular" or "academic" culture. Therefore, crafts learned in school or from books by people in suburban communities are in no way "folk crafts."

Source: D. C. Laubach (1989). Material folk culture. In *Introduction to folklore* (pp. 104–105). Portsmouth, NH: Boynton/Cook.

Every academic discipline has its key terms and concepts. When a new concept is introduced, the definition usually precedes any other discussion of the concept. Authors employ several strategies for defining a new concept.

- *Analysis of characteristics (both positive and negative):* The author lists several qualities of the term to separate it from other similar or related terms. The author often specifies both the qualities that the term exhibits and those that the term does not exhibit. For example:

  what

  Chinook winds are warm, dry winds that descend the eastern slope of the Rocky Mountains. They occur when strong westerly winds flow over a north-south mountain range, producing a trough of low pressure on the eastern side that forces the air downwards.

- *Analysis of function:* This strategy involves listing the purposes that a given term or concept serves within a larger framework (e.g., within an academic discipline, within society, within the physical world).

  why/how

  Civil inattention refers to the practice of strangers' ignoring each other when they pass by one another in a public place. This phenomenon occurs to make social interaction easier. It allows people to maintain their privacy and it reduces the need for extended politeness in public settings.

- *Analysis by example:* In this strategy, the author provides specific examples to illustrate and clarify a more general or abstract definition.

  for instance/example
  such as
  like

  Immigration involves the movement of individuals from one place to another, usually across political boundaries and for political, religious, and economic reasons. For example, many immigrants to the United States today come from war-torn Central America. However, the earliest immigrants to the United States, the Pilgrims, came seeking religious freedom and in the hopes of escaping the economic hardships imposed by the strict European class structure.

Sometimes authors combine these strategies to make new ideas as clear as possible.

Since extended definitions treat complex ideas, a simple dictionary definition is not enough. Instead, the writer presents more detail to help readers see (1) how the term fits into the larger topic being discussed and (2) what the writer's perspective on the term is.

TASK 8: The two excerpts from academic texts on page 6 are definitions of material folk culture. Indicate the definition strategies that each excerpt represents.

Definition 1: ~~Analysis of characteristics & Analysis by example~~ Analysis of function

Definition 2: ~~Analysis of function~~ Analysis of characteristics

TASK 9: What are the characteristics and functions of folk objects given in the two excerpts?

CHARACTERISTICS OF FOLK OBJECTS	FUNCTIONS OF FOLK OBJECTS
_____	_____
_____	_____
_____	_____
_____	_____
_____	_____

VIDEO

UNDERSTANDING THROUGH LISTENING

> **Lecture:** Folk Art
> **Segment 1:** What Is Folk Art?
>
> **Professor:** Donald Cosentino
> **Course:** Folklore 101: Introduction to Folklore
> **Text:** *Folk Groups and Folklore Genres* edited by Elliott Oring

In this lecture, Professor Donald Cosentino provides a brief definition of folk art.

TASK 10: While watching the lecture, jot down the main points. Based on your notes, decide which definition of folk art objects on page 6 most closely reflects Professor Cosentino's.

UNDERSTANDING THROUGH LITERATURE

In the reading on page 9, Thomas Whiterock, a Native American, explains his Navajo culture to a Vietnamese friend.

TASK 11: Focus on the Navajo folk objects Whiterock mentions as you read the passage.

MY NAVAJO HOME IN LOS ANGELES

Thomas Whiterock

[1]   On a warm summer day, my friend Tung and I walked into my mother's house. It was a relief to be out of the heat and to feel the coolness of home. I immediately began to walk across the living room to get to the stack of homework waiting for me. Out of the corner of my eye, I noticed that Tung was not behind me, but was still standing in the doorway, staring at the opposing wall. "What is that?" he asked, pointing to the wall. "That," I said, "is Navajo. Just look around, and you'll see Navajo items everywhere."

[2]   Across from where Tung stood hung a large painting of pottery and corn on a table top. The pottery, white and brown, is decorated with bold, black lines and birds. The corn is made up of vivid squares of white, yellow, maroon, brown, and black wrapped in pale husks. On one side of the painting is a bushel of "Indian" corn, the same as depicted in the painting. I explained that corn is as important to our diet as rice is to his. When the white man put us on reservations to change our religion and language, he also tried to change our food. We were given corn in equal rations with wheat, which was foreign to us. We had to fight for our corn. On the other side of the painting hangs a bushel of long, red chili peppers. The chili was introduced to us by the Spanish, but today is still consumed with each meal in most Navajo families.

[3]   Next, Tung pointed to the ladder leaning against the wall, a crude ladder made of bare wood. The rungs were held tightly in the notches with straps of leather. "Why do you have a ladder in the house?" he asked. "This, too, is Navajo," I explained. Though there were different kinds of houses, or hogans, the most common was the square, one-room house made of logs and adobe. These homes had lofts for the children to sleep in, and leading up to these lofts were ladders. Even though we had no loft, the ladder was here. The ladder was a relic of older times and a reminder of our heritage.

[4]   I then unfolded a rug that hung over the third rung. "This rug is purposely red," I said, "because red represents wisdom, which is very important in our culture." He then asked what the other rugs were for, referring to the rug on the table, the one on the couch and another on the wall. The colors have various meanings, depending on their use, I explained. The largest rug is turquoise, which represents spiritual goodness. The designs are of the "holy" people who will protect us. The black and red rug means knowledge, and the lines and diamond shapes are symbolic for corn stalks, which produce the main parts of our diet.

[5]   Together, we looked closely at the smaller painting on the side of the entry way to the dining room. One painting is of a Navajo woman weaving, a second is a child at play, and a third is a man herding sheep. Tung picked up the pottery from the shelf to get a closer look, but something else caught his eye. After putting the pottery down carefully, he slowly walked to the corner of the room and picked up the stick that lay there. The sound it made amazed him. He tilted the stick back and forth. This always holds the most fascination for guests, and it's something my family is used to explaining. I told him, "That is the cause of ignorant statements and stereotypes and makes us the butt of many jokes. But it also means much to my people." He moved it back and forth, listening. "Yes, there really is a rain dance," I continued. "Not like you see in cartoons or in old movies made by white men, though. This is a ceremony performed by the Zuni, the Hopi, and the Navajo. It was vital to their harvest." Tung was holding the rainstick used in the ceremony. The simulated sound of rainfall as the seeds rolling through the small tunnels of the hollow stick made Tung smile. "Put the stick down," I joked, "before it starts to rain."

[6]   Caught up in the excitement of explaining my culture that I walk by every day without noticing, I finally dragged Tung to the kitchen. I pointed to the sunflowers that are sprinkled around the room. I told him the story of the sunflowers' disappearance from our region for a few years, which was understood to be a bad sign. When the flower returned, it was proof that the spirits were happy with us. I pointed to the ceramic mushrooms on the table and on the counter and explained that they are used for visionquests or wisdomquests. I was on a roll! Before he could ask, I stepped quickly to the window and stood underneath a large, silk butterfly on the curtain. "This," I said, "represents two things in our art: dead warriors rising to the great hunting ground, and here," I paused to point to the butterfly, "the butterfly is taking our prayers to heaven."

[7]   I later walked Tung to the door after long hours of studying. He took another look around the room and smiled. "I like it here," he said. "It feels like a true home in every way." I opened the door. The sky had become overcast. It looked as if it just might rain after all.

Source: B. Lee (Ed.) (1995). *Celebrating diversity: A multi-cultural reader* (pp. 94–96). Lexington, MA: D.C. Heath.

TASK 12: List the objects found in the Navajo home and explain their significance. The first one has been completed for you.

OBJECT	SIGNIFICANCE
Painting of pottery and corn	Corn is the staple of the Navajo diet; the white man tried to change this food when Native Americans were put into reservations.
Learning against the wall	that's, too, is Navajo; there were different kinds of houses, or hogans, the most common was the square, one-room houses made of logs and adobe.
referring to the rug on the table	The colors have various meaning, depending their use

◉ Targeting Grammar: Fronting Adverb Phrases

Sentence order in English typically follows the pattern "Subject–Verb–Object" or "Subject–Verb–Adverb Phrase." An *adverb phrase* contains information about the manner, time, or location of the sentence's subject or verb.

Examples:

The Indians	weave	eye-dazzling rugs.
(subject)	(verb)	(object)

A bushel of Indian corn	stands	on one side of the painting.
(subject)	(verb)	(adverb phrase)

However, when the adverbial consists of a phrase indicating location, these elements can be *fronted*, or moved to initial position in the sentence:

Example:

On one side of the painting	stands	a bushel of Indian corn.
(adverb phrase)	(verb)	(subject)

Fronting of adverb phrases generally occurs for the following reasons:

1. to provide sentence variety
2. to orient the reader—spatially or in time
3. to move information you want to emphasize to the end of the sentence
4. to help sentences flow together in a paragraph
5. to give the language a more poetic flavor

TASK 13: Examine the following sentences taken from the readings in this unit. Rewrite each sentence so that it follows typical English word order.

1. Across from where Tung stood hung a large painting of pottery and corn on a table top.

_____

2. On one side of the painting is a bushel of "Indian" corn.

_____

3. On the other side of the painting hangs a bushel of long, red chili peppers.

_____

4. Propped in the center of the mantel is an old wall hanging.

_____

TASK 14: With another classmate, take turns describing aloud a familiar room or some other place that has a number of objects in it. The listener should take notes. When you are finished, write a paragraph on a separate piece of paper describing the room or place. Use one or two fronted adverb phrases of place similar to the examples in Task 13.

Integrating Perspectives

ANALYZING THROUGH DISCUSSION

In the poem below, the poet imagines that the reader is a bird alighting on the design of a Navajo rug or blanket. She describes the blanket and the feelings that the design evokes.

TASK 15: As you read the poem, underline all the words or phrases that describe the blanket.

A NAVAJO BLANKET

May Swenson

Eye-dazzlers the Indians weave. Three colors
are paths that pull you in, and pin you
to the maze. Brightness makes your eyes jump,
surveying the geometric field. Alight, and enter
any of the gates—of Blue, of Red, of Black.
Be calmed and hooded, a hawk brought down,
glad to fasten to the forearm of a Chief.

You can sleep at the center,
attended by Sun that never fades, by Moon
that cools. Then, slipping free of zigzag and
hypnotic diamond, find your way out
by the spirit trail, a faint Green thread that
secretly crosses the border, where your mind
is rinsed and returned to you like a white cup.

Source: (1994). *Nature: Poems old and new* (p. 192). Boston: Houghton Mifflin Co.

TASK 16: Below are the poet's phrases describing her reactions to the design of the blanket. For each original phrase, write a paraphrase of what you think the poet means. Use a dictionary if necessary. An example is done for you.

ORIGINAL PHRASE	PARAPHRASE
1. Eye-dazzlers the Indians weave.	1. The blankets fill viewers with wonder and admiration.
2. Three colors are paths that pull you in, and pin you to the maze.	2. Three colors make you inside
3. Alight, and enter any of the gates.	3. You can enter these gates
4. You can sleep at the center, attended by Sun that never fades, by Moon that cools.	4. You are not shone and dark, you are not along.
5. Slipping free of zigzag and hypnotic diamond, find your way out by the spirit trail.	5. Do whatever you want to do, you can be yourself.
6. Your mind is rinsed and returned to you. = through bad thing out	6. You are free.

TASK 17: Locate a folk art object (one that you own or have a picture of). Write a poem about this object by imitating Swenson's original poem. Use the partially completed poem below to guide you.

ORIGINAL POEM	YOUR POEM
Eye-dazzlers the Indians weave. Three colors are paths that pull you in, and pin you to the maze. **Brightness makes your eyes jump**, surveying the geometric field. Alight, and enter any of the gates—of Blue, of Red, of Black. **Be calmed and hooded, a hawk** brought down, glad to fasten to the forearm of a Chief.	Blankets the Indians make. Four colors are across that strange land and surprise you. These colors makes your eyes close. Be covered, like a maze.
You can sleep at the center, **attended by Sun that never fades**, by Moon that cools. **Then, slipping free of zigzag and hypnotic diamond, find your way out** by the spirit trail, a faint Green thread that secretly crosses the border, **where your mind is rinsed and returned** to you like a white cup.	You can use it on wherever attended by light that shines Then, keep your eyes on it you find some of them moved, where your mind/thinking to

EVALUATING THROUGH WRITING

One way to explore background knowledge about a topic is through journal writing. A *journal* is a personal record of experiences and reflections. In a journal entry, writers express their thoughts and feelings about a particular experience, concept, or idea. Despite the personal nature of most journal writing, students and teachers can use journals as a way to interact and share ideas.

ACADEMIC STRATEGY:

JOURNAL WRITING

TASK 18: Select one object from your home, or the home of a relative, that most reflects your culture. Write a journal entry in which you explain whether this object is an artifact of folk culture and why. Also discuss its cultural significance.

EXPLORATION:
RECOGNIZING CULTURE IN HANDMADE OBJECTS

Folk objects reflect a people's culture and values. The readings and lecture segments in this chapter show the interrelationship between folk objects and a people's culture and values. They also explain how, as cultural values change, the purpose, shape, and design of objects change to reflect shifts in world view. In other words, when we compare the same folk object from two different periods or two different cultures, we are able to trace differences in world view or culture.

Exploring the Concepts

EXPLORING THROUGH VISUAL IMAGES

Since death is an inevitable part of life, humans have probably been carving gravemarkers throughout their history. When researchers examine a culture's gravemarkers, they can learn much about the culture's values and beliefs.

TASK 1: Look at the two gravestone designs from seventeenth- and eighteenth-century Massachusetts below. What emotions about death does each gravemarker evoke? Which design would better represent your culture's view of death? Discuss these questions with a partner.

Gravestone Designs, Eastern Massachusetts

Death's Head (1678)   Winged Cherub (1759)

Task 2: What does each gravemarker convey about the culture's beliefs regarding God, death, and what an afterlife will be like? Write your ideas in the chart below.

	SEVENTEENTH CENTURY	EIGHTEENTH CENTURY
VIEW OF DIVINE BEING	God is an angry, punishing being.	God is sick, unhealth.
VIEW OF DEATH	Most people will die. When the people dead, after a couple of days the head will become skul	Death is a release from human suffering.
VIEW OF AN AFTERLIFE	You will very poor and have terrible life on the future.	You will go to ha happy, good and beautiful places.

Task 3: Based on what you can infer from the eighteenth-century gravemarker in Task 1, write a paragraph in which you summarize the culture's values surrounding death. The example of the seventeenth century has been done for you.

SEVENTEENTH CENTURY	EIGHTEENTH CENTURY
This culture believes in an afterlife. It fears its god and views the afterlife as a place where people are punished for the mistakes they made when they were alive.	This culture believes in diving being. You got horrible sick and you will dead. You look like unhappy. But after that you will go to other beautiful place.

EXPLORING THROUGH WRITING

One way of exploring an academic topic is first to see what personal connection it might have to our lives.

Task 4: Identify a folk object that is associated with a major life event (e.g., birth, marriage, death) in your culture. Write a journal entry about what this object shows about your culture's religious beliefs or world view.

Working with Sources

UNDERSTANDING THROUGH LISTENING 1

VIDEO

> **Lecture:** Folk Art
> **Segment 2:** Folk Art and World View
>
> **Professor:** Donald Cosentino
> **Course:** Folklore 101: Introduction to Folklore
> **Text:** *Folk Groups and Folklore Genres* edited by Elliott Oring

In this part of the lecture, Professor Cosentino discusses how world view, or *Weltanschauung,* — German word is reflected in a culture's folk objects. He gives examples of the Xhosa people of southern Africa, and seventeenth- and eighteenth-century gravemarkers in the United States.

ACADEMIC STRATEGY:

COPING WITH UNFAMILIAR WORDS IN ACADEMIC LECTURES

One strategy for dealing with academic terms you aren't familiar with is to keep a running list of these words in the margin of your lecture notes. Each time the word is repeated, place a √ next to your notation of it. If a word reoccurs several times, this should signal its importance. With repetitions and the contexts in which the repetitions occur, you may begin to form a clearer idea of the word's meaning. Multiple check marks next to a word should prompt you to look it up in a dictionary if its meaning is not clear to you by the end of the lecture. Even if you think you "sort of" understand the meaning of a word from the lecture context, it is a good idea to look it up after class to confirm your intuition.

To remember new vocabulary items and to make them a more active part of your own linguistic repertoire, you may want to keep a vocabulary notebook, using some of these strategies:

- Record no more than five words at a time; otherwise, you may not remember any of them.

- Divide your notebook into categories of words, such as words that you want to use actively in writing or speaking versus words that you only need to recognize and understand.

- Each entry should include the word, the definition, the part of speech (*adjective, adverb, noun, verb*, etc.), and the sentence context in which you first heard it.

- As much as possible, try to write your own definition of the word; don't simply copy down the dictionary definition—paraphrase it.

TASK 5: Below are some words that Professor Cosentino uses in his lecture. As you watch the lecture, put a √ under the appropriate column to indicate whether you already know this word or not. Also, put a √ in the column indicating whether the unknown words are important enough to look up after the lecture and to learn.

WORD	KNOWN	UNKNOWN	IMPORTANT?
iconography		✓	
secular representation		✓	✓
concretize		✓	
persistence		✓	✓
theology		✓	✓
preoccupation		✓	
elements		✓	✓
redefinition		✓	✓
enlightenment		✓	

Task 6: Choose five words from Task 5 that you consider important. Look them up in a dictionary and write a vocabulary notebook entry for each. An example has been done for you.

1. iconography
   Definition: artistic design
   Part of speech: noun
   Context: The seventeenth-century gravemarkers had certain designs; somewhere around 1750 this iconography changed.

2. _____

_____

_____

3. _____

_____

_____

4. _____

_____

_____

5. _____

_____

_____

Task 7: Watch the lecture again, concentrating on the contrast that Professor Cosentino makes between seventeenth- and eighteenth-century gravemarker designs and their meanings. Fill in the information you hear in the space provided. Does Professor Cosentino's information match the predictions you made in Task 2?

	SEVENTEENTH CENTURY	EIGHTEENTH CENTURY
DESCRIPTION OF THE GRAVEMARKER		
CONCEPT OF GOD		

TASK 8: Give an example of a folk art object that embodies or represents your culture's world view (or *Weltanschauung*). An example has been completed for you.

Quilts have been a part of American life since the country's beginnings. Because it is made from discarded scraps of fabric, the quilt represents the value of frugality and saving. Quilts have usually been made by groups of women at occasions known as quilting bees. Thus, the quilt also represents the high value placed on community and cooperation.

Targeting Vocabulary: Verbs Expressing Relationships

Academic texts often use certain verbs that express the relationship between a concept or object and its larger meaning or significance. For example, in the sentence "The roundness of Xhosa dwellings symbolizes the unbroken cycle of life," the verb *symbolize* indicates the type of relationship. Study the differences in meaning for each verb below. Notice that some meanings are overlapping and some show subtle differences.

reflect:	to express or to give an idea of something
express:	to show (a feeling, opinion, or fact) in words or some other way
represent:	to show; to be a sign or picture of; to stand for
signify:	to be a sign of; to mean; to express (especially an opinion) by an action
symbolize:	to represent or identify something by a symbol
mark:	to be a sign of
define:	to give the meaning of

Note: All of these verbs are transitive; that is, they are followed by a direct object, which, in this case, expresses the meaning of the verb. No preposition is used after the verb.

CONCRETE OBJECT OR CONCEPT	VERB EXPRESSING RELATIONSHIP	DIRECT OBJECT/MEANING
In some cultures, the shape of houses	defines	a world view.
The pattern of this patchwork quilt	symbolizes	the bonds of friendship.
A gift given to an eighteen-year-old	may mark	the transition to adulthood.
Folk art	reflects	a people's world view.

TASK 9: In the following sentences, replace the italicized verb with a verb that more appropriately links the concrete object or concept to its meaning. Choose another verb from the list on page 18. There may be more than one appropriate answer.

SENTENCE

MORE APPROPRIATE VERB

1. In the Navajo rug, the color red *defines* wisdom, an important part of Navajo culture.

   _____

2. Many people believe that the Puritan work ethic *expresses* American culture.

   _____

3. The silk butterfly on the curtain in Thomas Whiterock's house *marks* the rising of dead warriors to the great hunting ground.

   _____

4. The death's-head skulls on the gravemarkers of the seventeenth and eighteenth centuries *define* the view of an unforgiving divine being.

   _____

5. The nineteenth century and the American Enlightenment *express* a change in the way of thinking.

   _____

TASK 10: Match the object or concept in Column 1 with its meaning in Column 2. Then write a sentence in which you use the most appropriate verb to link the concrete objects or concepts to their meanings. The first has been completed as an example for you.

OBJECT OR CONCEPT	MEANING
material culture	significant field of study for historians
folk objects	a belief in a kind and forgiving God
folk art	a belief in a judgmental God
circular objects	*Weltanschauung*
death's-head skulls	a Xhosa way of seeing the world
happy little angels	world view

1. <u>Material culture reflects a people's world view.</u>

2. _____

3. _____

4. _____

5. _____

6. _____

UNDERSTANDING THROUGH READING

ACADEMIC STRATEGY:

HIGHLIGHTING OR MARKING A TEXT

One of the primary learning tools at the university is the academic textbook. Reading a textbook effectively requires the development of good reading habits. One such habit is *highlighting* or *marking* the important passages of the text.

Though readers may show some variation in what they highlight, most will mark the same key information and major points. Here are some tips for highlighting a text.

DO:
- Your first reading should be a quick reading for main ideas and supporting details. Do not mark the text at this point.
- On your second reading, use a marker to highlight main ideas, significant supporting information, and key terms.
- After your second reading, review what you have highlighted and mark or annotate it in the margins by adding your own stars, arrows, numbers, short written notes, or personal reactions.
- Make a list of key terms and ideas on a separate page for later review.

DON'T:
- Don't mark every sentence. Marking every sentence indicates that you can't decide what's important and you aren't thinking as you read.
- Don't leave a page without any marks; highlight or make a note about something on the page.
- Don't worry about ruining the book—it's yours to use as a learning tool.

In this article, Simon J. Bronner talks about what the details of folk objects reveal about the culture.

TASK 11: As you read the article, notice the main ideas and supporting ideas. With a highlighting pen, find and mark the main ideas in the passage.

FOLK OBJECTS, PART 1

Simon J. Bronner

[1]   The forms of folk objects are usually slow to change. Consequently, form becomes an especially good indicator of a historical region and its culture. Stone houses with the symmetrical form of one room on either side of a hallway and an elevation of one or two stories are so pervasive in Utah and surrounding areas that they place a distinctive mark upon the landscape. The distribution of this central-hall house and similar forms parallels the distribution of Mormon settlement in the West. Geographers see in the houses a visible and enduring imprint of a unique region of Mormon culture with sources in the Midwest and New England.

[2]   If the similarities of forms within a region indicate a shared culture, then the differences of basic forms may suggest differences of culture and world view. The bilateral symmetry of Utah's stone houses came into prominence as western society was increasingly transformed by science and technology in the late eighteenth century. To underscore human control over nature, the design of objects became less tied to natural forms. Surfaces were smoothed; their designs stressed frontal appearance; they relied more on the rectangle as a fundamental shape; they stood more erect. For the Navajo, who share the landscape with the Mormons in the Southwest, the more natural shape of the circle is the basic form in their houses, religious rituals, and art. Cultures that emphasize circles typically believe in a cycle of life rather than a linear span of years as western society does. Even the abstract notion of progress is given form in western society. Progress is often imagined as a line, moving upward or from left to right.

[3]   Unlike tales and songs, objects persist beyond the moment of their creation; they have an "objective existence." Indeed, the term "object" comes from the Latin for "throw." Objects are created by humans but once created, they stand apart. This difference between folk objects and other folklore genres has several consequences. One consequence is that objects have an obvious historical significance. Objects claim a historical character because they endure. They are intrusions from the past. Since folk objects commonly have to do with everyday life—the needs of shelter, work, prayer, and play—objects may help us to reexperience something of that everyday past.

[4]   One telling reminder of a life past is the gravemarker. In the cemeteries of eastern Massachusetts in the seventeenth and eighteenth centuries, three gravemarker designs predominate. Early stones, carved roughly between 1670 and 1760, show a winged death's head. By the mid-eighteenth century, winged cherubs replaced the grim visages of the skulls on the stones. By the end of the eighteenth century, the image of a willow tree overhanging a pedestaled urn appears, and in the early nineteenth century it quickly overtakes the cherub in popularity.

[5]   The life of late-seventeenth-century Puritanism is inscribed into the image of the death's head. Death's heads emphasize the mortality of man; accompanying symbols such as an hourglass or crossed bones underscore the brevity of life and quick decay in death. The imposing visage of the death's head reminded the Puritans of the severe judgment of a distant God who stood beyond the control or appeal of the individual. At the time when the winged cherubs appear, revivalist preachers such as Jonathan Edwards preached the individual's relationship with the deity; individuals felt they had more of a hand in the determination of their ultimate fate. The winged cherubs materialized the promise of heavenly reward and reflected the growing confidence in personal salvation. Accompanying the change to the willow and urn is a shift in form, for in this phase square shoulders replace the rounded shoulders of the stones carrying death's heads and winged cherubs. The squaring of the shoulders reflects a shifting attitude toward the significance of death and religious devotion. The new stones were markers of mourning, rather than doctrines of orthodoxy. Puritanism in Massachusetts at the time was giving way to new religions stressing individual intellect and volition, such as Unitarianism and Methodism, rather than community emotion and supernatural control. Death appeared less immediate; it had become an interruption of a full life. Emphasis changed from the supernatural status of the deceased to the secular mourning of the survivors.

[6]   Beliefs can also be communicated through objects. Material things can objectify ideas and feelings of fear, luck, or religious experience. Haunted houses are, in a sense, the objective correlatives of the fear and

wonder of the supernatural. For Pennsylvania Germans, the New Year's Day meal of pork and sauerkraut engenders good luck for the coming year. Among Jews, some mothers decorate a prayer shawl for their son's bar mitzvah. The shawl remains a visible and tangible reminder of the youth's status in the adult ritual community.

[7]   Because they stand apart from capricious humans, because their form seems fixed, because they can be seen and touched, and because they endure, objects appear reliable—indeed truthful. Seeing the object alone doesn't satisfy completely; reality comes from touching the object, feeling its three dimensionality. Rather than being accused of "seeing things" we want to be "in touch with reality." The truthfulness attached to objects is evinced by the biblical parable of "doubting Thomas." Thomas doubted Jesus Christ's resurrection until he had tactile proof. Until he could put his finger into the print of the nails and thrust his hand in Jesus's side, he would not be convinced. More recently, Apollo 10's close sighting of the moon failed to satisfy the American public; Neil Armstrong in Apollo 11 captured the imagination of the American public with his walk on the moon. The media glorified his grasp of a terrain at which we could formerly only look. The rocks Armstrong brought back held special fascination for the public because they could be touched, literally apprehended firsthand. Thus, objects can be used to confirm belief.

Source: E. Oring (Ed.) (1986). *Folk groups and folklore genres: An introduction* (pp. 199–223). Logan, UT: Utah State University Press.

TASK 12: Below are paraphrased versions of the main ideas in the text. Number these according to the order in which they appear.

___4___ Folk objects are tangible and, therefore, are taken as truths about a culture.

___2___ Similarities in the forms of folk objects demonstrate similar cultural values.

___7___ Because objects endure beyond human life, they have their own existence and thus carry historical significance.

___1___ Folk objects change form very gradually.

___6___ Folk objects communicate beliefs.

___3___ Differences in the forms of folk objects demonstrate differences in culture and world view.

TASK 13: Look again at your highlighting of the passage. Did the passages you marked as main ideas correspond to those given in Task 12? What other passages did you mark and why?

ACADEMIC STRATEGY:	Academic writers typically use examples to make a point or a generalization. Sometimes writers state the generalization they want the reader to draw.
USING EXAMPLES TO MAKE A GENERALIZATION	For example, in paragraph 7 of "Folk Objects, Part 1," the author gives two examples, the biblical example of "doubting Thomas" and the Apollo 11 example. The generalization the author draws is: "Thus, objects can be used to confirm belief."
	At other times, writers simply supply the examples and leave the reader to infer or guess at the generalization being made. An example of this strategy is found in paragraphs 4 and 5.

TASK 14: Reread paragraphs 4 and 5 of "Folk Objects, Part 1." List the examples given. What generalization do you believe the author wants you to draw about the significance of folk objects?

EXAMPLES	GENERALIZATION

Targeting Grammar: Using Adverbs of Frequency to Qualify a Generalization

In academic English, the following adverbs of frequency are used by writers to qualify or soften a general statement:

usually	often	commonly	seldom
typically	generally	frequently	occasionally

Example:

Cultures that emphasize circles **typically** believe in a cycle of life.

Without the adverb *typically* in the example sentence, the reader could interpret the statement to mean that *all* cultures emphasizing circles believe in a cycle of life; however, the addition of the adverb softens this statement and makes it less absolute. The reader should then interpret the statement to mean that *most* or *almost all* cultures that emphasize circles believe in a cycle of life.

We generally place adverbs of frequency in one of the following sentence positions:

- Before the main verb if there are no auxiliaries:

  Cultures that emphasize circles **typically** *believe* in a cycle of life.
                                             (main verb)

- After the first auxiliary if the verb has an auxiliary:

  Folklorists *have* **often** *used* folk objects to learn a culture's values.
     (auxiliary)   (main verb)

- After *be* if it is the main verb:

  The forms of folk objects *are* **usually** slow to change.
                   (be)

4. Describe the marker that you would place on your own grave. Explain what others would learn about your beliefs and values by looking at this gravemarker.

Just as each paragraph in an academic essay has one main idea (or topic sentence), the essay itself has a main idea, expressed in the form of a *thesis statement*. A thesis statement clearly lays out the author's intent in writing the piece and often gives an indication of the organizational pattern that the author will use. In academic writing, the thesis often comes at the end of the introductory paragraph(s) after the background information has been presented. Readers expect that the writer will develop the essay based on the information contained in the thesis statement.

EXAMPLE:

In "Folk Objects, Part 2" Bronner's purpose in writing the essay is to explain the relationship between humans and the objects in their environment. In the last sentence of the following paragraph, he clearly states his point of view—that humans project their ideas and emotions onto objects:

> Although objects stand apart, their relations with their human creators and owners are still recognizable. Human characteristics are attributed to object forms, so that chairs are described as having legs, lamps as having necks, and clocks as having faces. Some individuals interact with objects as though they were people. They give them names, talk to them, and decorate or "dress" them. In American culture, for example, cars are regularly named or personalized with special license plates or paint jobs. They may be praised for good performance or cursed for bad. Some individuals conceptualize the purchase of new mats, covers, or ornaments as buying "gifts" for their cars. **So,** despite the "otherness" of objects, **humans** nevertheless **project their own ideas and emotions onto them and see them as reflections of themselves.**

Readers of Bronner's essay expect from this thesis statement that the rest of his essay will develop this concept with examples and details that support his point of view.

MODEL:

For essay topic 1, a possible thesis statement might be:

> This teenager has surrounded himself with tapes, musical instruments, and music posters that reflect the importance of rock music and its anti-establishment values in his life.

This thesis statement promises several things and suggests a two-part outline that the essay will follow: the writer will describe the room in more detail and the connection between music and anti-establishment values will be further developed. Note that verbs such as *reflect*, *express*, *represent*, *mark*, and *signify* are useful in developing a thesis statement.

INSIGHTS FROM ATMOSPHERIC SCIENCES

INTRODUCTION:

LOCAL WINDS

One focus of the atmospheric sciences is the study of thermal circulations, commonly referred to as local winds. This chapter examines the phenomenon of local winds from a variety of perspectives including personal experience.

Exploring the Concepts

EXPLORING THROUGH VISUAL IMAGES

This picture is one artist's fanciful view of the wind. The artist has captured the force and power that the wind exerts on our lives.

TASK 1: Imagine that you are describing this picture to someone who hasn't seen it. What words would you use to convey how the artist sees the wind? Describe the picture orally in small groups.

EXPLORING BACKGROUND KNOWLEDGE

ACADEMIC STRATEGY: **CUBING**	To help develop an idea and expand on background knowledge, writers often use a technique called *cubing*, or examining a concept from many different perspectives. This is one way to brainstorm knowledge on a topic. Just as a cube has many different sides, a topic, such as wind, can be examined from several points of view.

TASK 2: Use the cube below to organize what you know about wind. Discuss each category with your classmates.

WIND

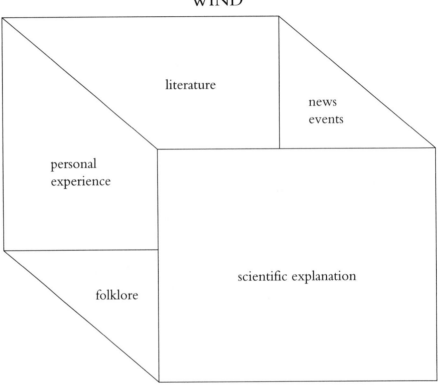

EXPLORING THROUGH WRITING

TASK 3: Select one aspect of your examination of wind. In your journal, write a one-paragraph description of your knowledge in this area.

⊚ Targeting Vocabulary: Expressing Power through Verbs

The literature and journal excerpts that follow in Working with Sources contain many verbs that characterize the power of wind.

TASK 4: Look over the verbs in the following chart. Each one has certain effects associated with it. For example, a wind that *uproots* has the power to pull plants or trees out of the ground. Explain the effects of each verb in the column on the right. Refer to a dictionary if necessary. The first one has been done for you.

	EFFECTS
1. uproot	pull something out of the ground by the roots
2. overturn	
3. smash	
4. toss	
5. splinter	
6. smack	
7. skim	
8. rip	

TASK 5: Expand the list of verbs through discussion with your classmates. Add words that express the effects of the wind.

Working with Sources

UNDERSTANDING THROUGH LITERATURE

The following excerpt from *A Year in Provence* by Peter Mayle describes the mistral, a cold wind that blows through the Rhône valley in southern France.

TASK 6: As you read the passage on page 48, locate the verbs listed in Task 4 and underline them.

A Year in Provence

Peter Mayle

[1]   Meanwhile, a thousand miles to the north, the wind that had started in Siberia was picking up speed for the final part of its journey. We had heard stories about the Mistral. It drove people, and animals, mad. It was an extenuating circumstance in crimes of violence. It blew for fifteen days on end, uprooting trees, overturning cars, smashing windows, tossing old ladies into the gutter, splintering telegraph poles, moaning through houses like a cold and baleful ghost, causing *la grippe,* domestic squabbles, absenteeism from work, toothache, migraine—every problem in Provence that couldn't be blamed on the politicians was the fault of the *sâcré vent . . . .*

[2]   [W]e were poorly prepared when the first Mistral of the year came howling down the Rhône valley, turned left, and smacked into the west side of the house with enough force to skim roof tiles into the swimming pool and rip a window that had carelessly been left open off its hinges. The temperature dropped twenty degrees in twenty-four hours. It went to zero, then six below. Readings taken in Marseilles showed a wind speed of 180 kilometers an hour. My wife was cooking in an overcoat. I was trying to type in gloves. We stopped talking about our first swim and thought wistfully about central heating. And then one morning, with the sound of branches snapping, the pipes burst one after the other under the pressure of water that had frozen in them overnight.

Source: (1991). *A year in Provence* (pp. 8–9). New York, NY: Vintage Press.

---

la grippe—the flu, *sâcré vent*—cursed wind

TASK 7: For each of the verbs you underlined in Task 6, identify the object that is affected by this action. The first one has been done for you.

ACTION	OBJECT
1. uproot	trees
2. overturn	
3. smash	
4. toss	
5. splinter	
6. smack	
7. skim	
8. rip	

Targeting Grammar: Participial Phrases

A participle is a verb form ending in *-ing* that is sometimes used as an adjective. Writers often use participial phrases in description. As verb forms, participles express action and therefore intensify a descriptive passage. Look at the following sentences from *A Year in Provence.* Note the effect that the participial phrases have on the description.

It blew for fifteen days on end, **uprooting** trees, **overturning** cars, **smashing** windows, **tossing** old ladies into the gutter, **splintering** telegraph poles, **moaning** through houses like a cold and baleful ghost, **causing** *la grippe,* domestic squabbles, absenteeism from work, toothache, migraine—every problem in Provence that couldn't be blamed on the politicians was the fault of the **sâcré vent.**

Notice that in this excerpt, all of the participial phrases are formed from the *-ing* form, or present participle.

Participial phrases often modify the subject of the sentence. In the following examples, the participial phrases modify the subject *wind*.

> The wind blew for fifteen days on end, **uprooting trees and overturning cars.**
> **Uprooting trees and overturning cars,** the wind blew for fifteen days on end.

Participial phrases at the beginning of sentences are usually set off by commas. They are also often set off by commas at the end of sentences when they modify the subject.

If a participial phrase is placed before the subject but does not modify the subject, it is incorrect. This type of error is called a *dangling modifier.*

> **Uprooting trees and overturning cars, *I*** was frightened by the wind.
> (Incorrect: *I* did not uproot trees and overturn cars: the *wind* did)
> **Uprooting trees and overturning cars, *the wind*** frightened me.
> (Correct: The *wind* uprooted trees and overturned cars.)

TASK 8: For each sentence below, underline the participial phrase once and the subject twice. Then identify whether the participial phrase is used correctly. Put a check mark in the appropriate column. The first one has been done for you.

	CORRECT	INCORRECT
1. <u>Picking up speed,</u> <u><u>the wind</u></u> splintered telegraph poles and ripped off windows.	√	
2. Dropping twenty degrees in twenty-four hours, the temperature eventually hit six below.		
3. Typing in gloves, I tried to keep my hands warm.		
4. Bursting under the pressure of the frozen water, I called a plumber to fix the pipes.		
5. Moaning like a ghost, the wind picked up speed for the final part of its journey.		
6. Thinking wistfully about central heating, the wind speed reached 180 kilometers an hour.		

TASK 9: Many geographic regions have local wind systems that affect the lifestyle of the people there. Think for a moment about an area that you are familiar with. What are the wind patterns like? Write a brief journal entry in which you describe the local wind system for that area. Use *-ing* participial phrases to intensify your description.

UNDERSTANDING THROUGH READING 1

The following is excerpted from an article on the south of France from a popular travel magazine, the *Condé Nast Traveler*.

TASK 10: Before you read Clive Irving's experiences with a local wind called the *mistral*, look back at the cube diagram you completed in Task 2 (page 46) to remind yourself of the personal experiences about wind you brainstormed.

RELISH THE RHÔNE

Clive Irving

[1]   It began with a furtive rattling of the window shutters and a faint howling around the medieval casements. Night sounds where there had been many night sounds through the ages. By morning the howling was incessant. I pushed open the shutters against a forcefully resistant wind.

[2]   This was a pervasive, inhabiting wind. It raged across the hill above, tearing into freshly bloomed cascades of yellow broom so that the color writhed. Cypresses, the most exposed of the trees, flexed acutely in the line of the wind. They signaled its direction—and identity. The intruder came from the north, sucked down the great valley of the Rhône and into Provence like a jet stream. This was the mistral.

[3]   The evening before had been different, a foretaste of summer in a backwater of southern France called Drome-Provençal. I had followed a minor tributary of the Rhône, the Jabron, into a valley and to a medieval village called Le Poët-Laval. There, on a hillside, I found a commandery originally built by those ardent Christian hosts, the Knights of Malta, in the fourteenth century. The commandery is now a hotel, Les Hospitaliers. Dinner on the terrace overlooking the Jabron Valley had been serene. A light, warm breeze wafted up its scents: lavender, lime (the *tilleul*, whose fresh blossoms are locally dried for use in a soothing herb tea), broom, and even the ripe cherries that hung heavy in the orchards below.

[4]   Then came the mistral to remind us that Mother Nature can be a spoiler, too.

[5]   My memory of the mistral was of something warmer and more congenial. It had been many years earlier in the crucible of the southern Midi, at Carcassonne. Then the wind had been at my back, urging me on to Spain while it remained domiciled in France. With enduring luck, I had never felt it again.

[6]   Until now. The concierge at Les Hospitaliers admitted that it was unusually late in the spring for the mistral to strike, and offered with mathematical certainty that it would last for either three, six, or nine days.

[7]   I checked with a more scientific source. A mistral is generated when two vast rotations of pressure converge: high pressure over the mountains and plateaus west of the Rhône and, to the east, a low-pressure storm system over the Alps and northern Italy. The Rhône valley acts as a funnel between these two systems, drawing down cold, desiccating air from the Alps. The wind can be miles high, and it gathers force as it roars toward its nemesis, the Mediterranean.

[8]   I could see one effect immediately. The sky was rinsed clean of haze. This produced a stark, intense light that seemed to curb or even eradicate shadows. Where there was shade it was suddenly chill. This polarization of light and temperature driven by violence was, I suddenly realized, very familiar—it invests the final landscapes of Vincent van Gogh.

[9]   The blaze of colors he found when he arrived in Provence was not inert, and his olive trees have the gnarled ligaments that come from fighting the mistral year after year.

[10]   The mistral is a living force, blowing grit in your face and perspective into your vision. It shapes the lands of the Rhône as profoundly as history.

Source: (1995, May). *Condé Nast Traveler*, 142.

⊙ Targeting Grammar: Verb Tense in Description Narration, and Explanation

In "Relish the Rhône," Irving describes his experiences, using the past and past perfect tenses. However, when explaining the phenomenon of the *mistral*, he shifts to the present tense. The rules below provide basic guidelines for the use of these tenses.

1. The *simple present* is used to express general statements of fact and habitual activity. It is often used when providing scientific explanations such as those found in academic textbooks. Its purpose is to explain.

    The mistral **is** a living force . . . it **shapes** the lands of the Rhône as profoundly as history.

2. The *simple past* is used to describe an event that was completed at a specific time in the past. Its purpose is to describe or narrate past events.

    By morning the howling **was** incessant. I **pushed open** the shutters against a forcefully resistant wind.

3. The *past perfect* is used to describe an event that happened before another event in the past. Often, it is used in conjunction with the simple past tense. Its purpose is to indicate a sequence of events in the past.

    The evening before, the howling of the wind **had been** faint. By morning, the howling **was** incessant.

Look at the following excerpt from "Relish the Rhône" and note how the writer has switched tenses to reflect the order of events in this narration.

> I **had followed** a minor tributary of the Rhône, the Jabron, into a valley and to a medieval village called Le Poët-Laval. There, on a hillside, I **found** a commandery originally built by those ardent Christian hosts, the Knights of Malta, in the fourteenth century. The commandery **is** now a hotel, Les Hospitaliers. Dinner on the terrace overlooking the Jabron Valley **had been** serene.

TASK 11: For each sentence below, decide the tense of each verb (present, simple past, or past perfect) and what the writer's purpose is (to describe/narrate a past event, to explain, or to indicate a sequence of events in the past). The first one has been done for you.

SENTENCE	TENSE	PURPOSE
1. The intruder came from the north.	simple past tense	to describe/narrate
2. A light warm breeze wafted up its scents.		
3. The Rhône Valley acts as a funnel.		
4. This produced a stark, intense light.		
5. It gathers force as it roars toward its nemesis, the Mediterranean.		
6. Where there was shade it was suddenly chill.		
7. The evening before had been different.		

TASK 12: One paragraph in "Relish the Rhône" provides a scientific explanation of the *mistral*. Identify this paragraph and list the present tense verbs that you find.

_____   _____   _____

_____   _____   _____

_____   _____   _____

VIDEO

UNDERSTANDING THROUGH LISTENING

> **Lecture:** Introduction to Atmospheric Environments
> **Segment 1:** Wind Direction
>
> **Professor:** Jeffrey Lew
> **Course:** Atmospheric Science 3: Introduction to Atmospheric Environments
> **Text:** *Essentials of Meteorology* by C. Donald Ahrens

In the following lecture segment, Professor Jeffrey Lew explains wind direction and wind names.

TASK 13: Watch the entire lecture segment and take notes on the main ideas. Then answer these questions.

1. What is a wind vane?

_____

2. Which direction does a northeast wind come from?

_____

3. Which direction does a northeast wind blow to?

_____

ACADEMIC STRATEGY:

COMPREHENDING UNSTRESSED WORDS

English is a *stress-timed* language. This means that certain words in a sentence (the *content words*) receive heavier emphasis. These words include nouns, main verbs, adjectives, and adverbs. In the sentence below from Professor Lew's lecture, the content words appear in bold because they are the stressed elements.

The **wind vane** is **used** to **get** the **direction** of the **wind.**

Other words in the sentence (the *function words*) are unstressed. These function words include prepositions, articles, conjunctions, and auxiliary verbs. Because these words are unstressed, they can be difficult to hear. However, they are grammatically important to understanding the meaning of the sentence. Look again at the example sentence above. Notice that if Professor Lew had said "Wind vane used get direction wind" the sentence would be difficult to comprehend. This is because the grammatical relationships between the content words are expressed through the function words.

When you listen to a lecture, you will probably notice the content words most easily and will tend to write down more content words in your lecture notes than function words. This is because we can use our knowledge of English grammar to fill in the "missing pieces" as we review our lecture notes. Similarly, when we listen to spoken language, we rely on our knowledge of English grammar to fill in the elements of the sentence that are unstressed.

TASK 14: Read the incomplete passages below. Before watching the lecture segment again, use your knowledge of English grammar to predict the unstressed words that are missing. As you hear each passage, check your predictions and correct those that were incorrect.

1. _____ direction _____ the wind is said _____ be the direction from which _____ wind is blowing.

2. If _____ wind is blowing from left _____ right, _____ from west to east, then we say that this is _____ west wind.

3. _____ wind which is blowing from _____ upper right corner _____ the lower left corner is coming _____ the northeast, so we call that _____ northeast wind.

4. This instrument here _____ actually a combination windvane _____ and a wind speed measuring device.

5. The head _____ the windvane here _____ actually point against the wind _____ will point toward _____ direction from which _____ wind _____ going.

6. It always points into _____ wind because the wind does not push _____ head around, it pushes the tail around, so if the wind were coming from here to here _____ let's say the vane happened _____ be pointing this way, it'll hit the tail _____ this and then will point _____ the direction from which the wind _____ coming from.

7. You _____ use decorative windvanes _____ they'll accomplish _____ same thing.

UNDERSTANDING THROUGH READING 2

The following reading is taken from *Weatherwise*, a magazine for people who are interested in the weather. The passage describes popular beliefs held in many parts of the world about wind.

TASK 15: Look back at the cube diagram you completed in Task 2 (page 46) to review the wind folklore and mythology you are familiar with.

TASK 16: Before reading, fill in the diagram below with any ideas or background knowledge that you have associated with each direction of the wind.

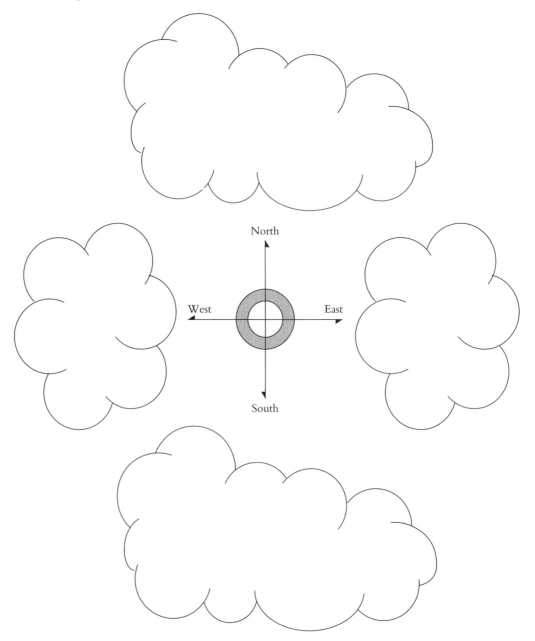

Demon's Gates and Devil's Doors

Mary Reed

[1]   A legendary poem, "Winds of Fate," describes the pagan Irish belief that the wind's direction at birth foretells a person's future. The bard, who's long since passed into obscurity, wrote that the west wind brings a simple life, the south wind brings luxury and many friends, the north wind makes a boy a warrior, and the east wind comes laden with riches. A person born during a dead calm, the poem says, is destined to be a fool. While one may dismiss the wind as nothing more than a refreshing breeze or a warning of an imminent deluge, the Irish are not alone in giving the wind and its direction credit for more than just the weather.

[2]   Generally speaking, the north wind is the gloomiest of the four, usually bringing wet, cold weather. In some European mythologies the north wind was strongly connected with death and the afterlife. In European folklore the north itself is considered in a bad light. In fact, one saying goes so far as to assert that only bad things originate there, listing in particular frosts, cutting winds, and a scold for the wife! Slavs connect the north with the darkness of midnight, curiously echoed in the Algonquin belief that the north winds come from black, cold lands.

[3]   The north entrance of an English church is traditionally called the "devil's door," and is occasionally left open during baptisms as an escape route for evil. The Japanese also consider the north an extremely ill-favored direction and prefer not to have their houses face that way, although so-called "demon's gates" in the garden are so oriented as a protective measure. Buddhists have protectresses for each of the four directions. The north protects against snake bites, which is good news for Japanese Buddhists who enjoy gardening.

[4]   All is not ill for the north wind, however, for because of its cooling effect, the ancient Egyptians referred to it in one of their Pharaoh's many titles: "Lord of the Sweet Breeze." This kind regard for the north wind is no doubt based upon geographical rather than cultural differences, for the Old Testament's Job (37:22) also mentions that "fair weather cometh out of the north."

[5]   The north wind is also said to sharpen men's appetites, but not for fish, it is hoped. A traditional rhyme advises fishermen to avoid going out when the wind is in that quarter, for it will blow the bait out of piscean mouths, to which one might add a caution about the possibilities of catching a chill rather than a chub in such weather.

[6]   The south wind traditionally promotes a slowing of life's tempo. Known generally in Europe as a rain bearer, the south wind of the Athenian Temple of the Winds carries a downward-tilting water jar in homage to this. The Greek philosopher Theophrastus was of the opinion that south winds "froze" the joints, whereas the north wind, quite in reverse to what one might have expected, balanced the fluidity of the joints, causing both ease of, and powerful, movements.

[7]   The south wind usually has been connected with summer and good harvests, and thus is a fortunate wind, but despite its gentle reputation, it was symbolized in the East as a winged lion with four heads, or one of a quartet of winged leopards. In a native American folk tale, the south wind was said to interfere with hunting.

[8]   The east probably is the most disliked of the winds. The ancients thought it harmed crops, and around the Mediterranean it had a bad reputation for causing shipwrecks. According to one traditional rhyme, the east wind blows rain back to the west—not necessarily a good thing in dry summers. Eric Sloane, in his *Folklore of American Weather* (Duell, Sloane, and Pearce, 1963), likens it to a "boring guest that hasn't enough sense to leave." In Greece, however, the east wind is a rainbringer and is represented on the Temple of the Winds as a young man laden with the fruits of the earth.

[9]   The east, both the compass point and the geopolitical region, has always been connected with spiritual matters and rebirth. Statues in many temples are situated to be gilded by the golden rays of the rising sun. On the other hand, Mentu, the Egyptian god of the rising sun (and the breather of life into newborns), was also their god of war.

[10]   By contrast, no less an authority than the U.S. government declared in the first edition of the Department of Agriculture's *Weather Book,* that west winds are "fair weather winds." Alas, to Homer the western sea winds conjured up by Poseidon, god of the sea, were stormy. This, however, was an aspect of advantage to the Egyptians, whose plague of locusts was blown away by winds from that quarter (Exodus 10:19).

[11]   Traditionally in Europe the west wind offered the best time for fishing, for it was said to blow the bait into fish's mouths, thus ensuring a good catch. Wily Ben Franklin advised conducting business when western winds blew, presumably because this was usually a time of good weather when both the barometer and men's spirits were high.

[12]   Doubtless because it is into the west that the sun sinks, the direction has long been connected with death and the afterlife, and in many mythologies the world over it is where Paradise—often a land of summer, fruitful and warm—is situated. Thus the west has its melancholy aspects as well as its gentler connections. No doubt the Irish bard who wrote "Winds of Fate" may be said to have gone with the wind, almost certainly a western one.

Source: (1993/4, December/ January). *Weatherwise*, 38–39.

TASK 17: After reading "Demon's Gates and Devil's Doors," return to the diagram about the four winds that you filled out in Task 16 (page 54). What information can you add? Compare the diagram with your classmates'.

Targeting Grammar: Expressing Contrast through Subordination

CONTRAST WITH THE COORDINATING CONJUNCTION *BUT*

One of the most common ways to express contrast is to connect two *independent clauses* (each with its own subject and verb) with the coordinating conjunction *but*.

A person who is born during a dead calm is a fool
(subject)   (verb)

but

a person who is born during a south wind is fortunate.
(subject)   (verb)

CONTRAST WITH THE SUBORDINATING CONJUNCTIONS *WHILE, WHEREAS, ALTHOUGH*

Contrast is also expressed through dependent clauses introduced by the subordinating conjunctions *while*, *whereas*, and *although*. The dependent clause does not express a complete thought and must be connected to an independent clause to avoid sentence fragments.

While the west wind brings simple life, the south wind brings luxury.
        (dependent clause)   (independent clause)

People born during a north wind are destined to be warriors **whereas** people born
                        (independent clause)   (dependent clause)
during a dead calm become fools.

Study the possible patterns for each of these subordinating conjunctions. Notice how the punctuation changes.

Pattern A:

| subordinating conjunction + dependent clause | , | independent clause |

Although the west wind brings a simple life, the south wind brings luxury.

Pattern B:

| independent clause | + | subordinating conjunction + dependent clause |

The west wind brings a simple life **whereas** the south wind brings luxury.

Both Pattern A and Pattern B above are useful patterns for expressing contrast in academic writing. Using both these patterns adds variety to your writing.

Task 18: Match the information from column B with the contrasting information in column A. Then, using the subordinating conjunctions *while*, *whereas*, and *although*, write sentences showing contrast. Vary the sentence patterns and subordinating conjunctions. The first one has been done for you.

COLUMN A

___e___ 1. The north wind brings wet, cold weather and is considered an ill-favored direction.

_____ 2. For the ancient Greeks, the south wind was believed to "freeze" the joints.

_____ 3. For the Americans, west winds are considered fair-weather winds.

_____ 4. The north wind is considered the gloomiest of the winds.

_____ 5. It is generally believed that the east wind chases rain away.

_____ 6. Europeans avoid fishing when the north wind is blowing.

COLUMN B

a. The north wind loosened the joints and caused ease of movement.

b. The south wind usually has been connected with summer and is thus viewed as a fortunate wind.

c. The ancient Egyptians considered the north wind a "sweet wind."

d. In Greece, the east wind is a rain bringer.

e. The blowing of the west wind is thought to ensure good fishing.

f. For the ancient Greeks, west winds brought storms.

1.   While the north wind brings wet, cold weather and is considered an ill-favored direction, the south wind usually has been connected with summer and is thus viewed as a fortunate wind.

2.   _____

_____

3.   _____

_____

4.   _____

_____

5.   _____

_____

6.   _____

_____

Integrating Perspectives

APPLYING THE CONCEPTS

ACADEMIC STRATEGY: SENSORY DESCRIPTION IN STORYTELLING	*Oral history,* or the art of storytelling, was one way for people to pass knowledge from one generation to another. Some stories took the form of folklore or myths and, with each successive generation, became more embellished and descriptive. "Demon's Gates and Devil's Doors" contains many such myths and folktales. These types of stories tend to be colorful, employing highly descriptive language that appeals to the senses of sight, sound, touch, taste, and smell. To create these sensory images, authors select vivid adjectives and verbs.

TASK 19: Identify the descriptive language in the phrases below by determining which of the senses (sight, smell, sound, taste, touch) is being appealed to and how the author is making this appeal. Discuss your responses with your partners. The first one has been done for you.

SOURCE PHRASE	SENSE	MANNER OF APPEAL
1. We were poorly prepared when the first Mistral of the year came howling down the Rhône Valley. (*A Year in Provence,* paragraph 2)	sound	*word choice:* howl is a word describing the type of sound made by the wind.
2. It blew for fifteen days on end, uprooting trees, overturning cars, smashing windows, tossing old ladies into the gutter. (*A Year in Provence,* paragraph 1)		
3. It began with a furtive rattling of the window shutters and a faint howling around the medieval casements. ("Relish the Rhône," paragraph 1)		
4. The north wind is also said to sharpen men's appetites, but not for fish, it is hoped. ("Demon's Gates and Devil's Doors," paragraph 5)		
5. The Greek philosopher Theophrastus was of the opinion that south winds "froze" the joints. ("Demon's Gates and Devil's Doors," paragraph 6)		

ANALYZING THROUGH DISCUSSION

TASK 20: Working in small groups, describe an experience you have had with wind or weather. Appeal to your audience's senses by employing the many types of creative language discussed in this chapter. What suggestions can you make to enhance your classmates' descriptions?

EVALUATING THROUGH WRITING

TASK 21: Write a descriptive essay in which you elaborate upon your wind or weather experiences. Pay close attention to word selection by using a thesaurus when necessary. Also try to incorporate the various elements of descriptive writing featured in this chapter.

EXPLORATION: THERMAL CIRCULATIONS

The focus of this chapter is thermal circulation patterns. Sea and land breezes, mountain and valley breezes, katabatic winds, chinook winds, and other systems are explained through academic lectures and readings.

Exploring the Concepts

EXPLORING THROUGH VISUAL IMAGES

ACADEMIC STRATEGY:

PREVIEWING ILLUSTRATIONS IN A TEXT

One important step in previewing a text is to look at the diagrams, charts, and illustrations before reading. This allows the reader to develop a working understanding of the processes and details in the text.

TASK 1: Look at the figures below. What processes are being illustrated? Working with a partner, explain what is taking place in each figure.

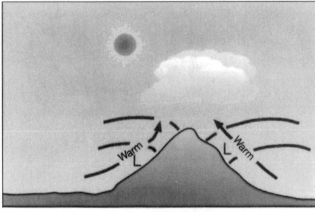

Valley Breeze

Figure 1

Mountain Breeze

Figure 2

☀ Targeting Vocabulary: Geographical Terms

TASK 2: The readings that follow contain many references to geographical terms. Look over the diagrams below. Match the term from the list with the appropriate diagram. Use a dictionary if necessary.

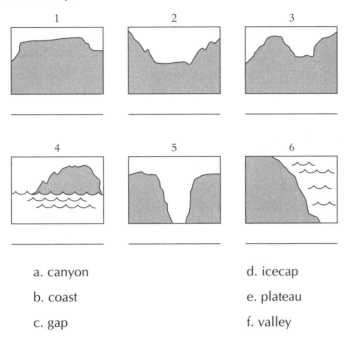

a. canyon

b. coast

c. gap

d. icecap

e. plateau

f. valley

EXPLORING THROUGH DISCUSSION

Below is a photo of the Grand Canyon, located in northern Arizona.

TASK 3: With a partner or a small group, discuss what role wind and the other elements (e.g., water, glaciers, earthquakes) might have played in the creation of this geographical feature.

Exploring through Writing

Wind patterns can be a factor in the creation of geographical features (e.g., a plateau). Conversely, the geographical feature (e.g., a mountain range) can also affect the thermal circulation pattern.

Task 4: Think of a local geographical feature (e.g., a plateau, a canyon) in a place you are familiar with. In your journal, write a paragraph describing this feature. Include a comment about the connection between this feature and wind. For example, you may want to discuss how wind helped to create this feature or how wind patterns are associated with the feature.

Working with Sources

Understanding through Reading 1

In "Local Wind Systems," the author defines thermal circulations, discussing the two types of circulation: land/sea and mountain/valley.

Academic Strategy: **Previewing an Academic Text**

Good academic readers *preview* a text, or look over the text completely, before they begin reading it in depth. There are several purposes for previewing an academic text:

- It activates the reader's background knowledge so that new information can be connected to previously known information.
- It provides the reader with a sense of the author's purpose in writing the text.
- It provides the reader with a sense of the global organization of the text so the reader can process the text more quickly.
- It helps the reader make decisions about what to focus on in terms of the main information contained in the text.
- With longer texts (e.g., textbook chapters), it helps the reader make decisions about how much time it will take to read the text and how to manage this time most efficiently.

To preview a text, do the following:

- Read the headings and subheadings of the text. These provide you with a sense of the text's global organization.
- Read the first and last paragraph of the passage. These paragraphs often contain the author's purpose and a summary of the main points.
- Read the first and last sentence of each paragraph. These usually contain the paragraph's topic sentence and its conclusion.

- Look at any charts, graphs, and pictures contained in the reading. These visuals often represent key information from the text or add examples to clarify the text.
- Formulate questions about the content of the passage that you think will be answered in the text itself. As you reread, try to answer these questions in your mind.

TASK 5: Before reading, take a few minutes to preview the text. Briefly answer the following questions on separate paper:

1. How many paragraphs are in this reading?

2. Identify the headings. What do these tell you about the topic of this reading?

3. What do you already know about this topic?

4. What do you want to learn about this topic?

TASK 6: The author organizes the following reading about local wind systems by contrasting wind characteristics during the day and at night. As you read, focus on this contrast and pay attention to the conditions that affect changes in wind direction.

LOCAL WIND SYSTEMS

C. Donald Ahrens

Thermal Circulations

[1]   We will begin our study of local winds by examining the formation of thermal circulations. Circulations brought on by changes in air temperature, in which warmer air rises and colder air sinks, are termed thermal circulations. As cool surface air flows southward, it warms and becomes less dense. In the region of surface low pressure, the warm air slowly rises, expands, cools, and flows out the top at an elevation of about one kilometer (3300 feet) above the surface. At this level, the air flows horizontally northward toward lower pressure, where it completes the circulation by slowly sinking and flowing out the bottom of the surface high.

[2]   The regions of the surface high and low atmospheric pressure created as the atmosphere either cools or warms are called *thermal highs* and *thermal lows*. In general, they are shallow systems, usually extending no more than a few kilometers above the ground.

Sea and Land Breezes

[3]   The sea breeze is a type of thermal circulation. The uneven heating rates of land and water cause these mesoscale coastal winds. During the day, the land heats more quickly than the adjacent water, and the intensive heating of the air above produces a shallow thermal low. The air over the water remains cooler than the air over the land; hence, a shallow thermal high exists above the water. The overall effect of this pressure distribution is a sea breeze that blows from the sea toward the land. Since the strongest gradients of temperature and pressure occur near the land-water boundary, the strongest winds typically occur right near the beach and diminish inland. Further, since the greatest contrast in temperature between land and water usually occurs in the afternoon, sea breezes are strongest at this time. (The same type of breeze that develops along the shore of a large lake is called a *lake breeze*.)

[4]   At night, the land cools more quickly than the water. The air above the land becomes cooler than the air above the water, producing a distribution of pressure. With higher surface pressure now over the land, the wind reverses itself and becomes a land breeze—a breeze that flows from the land toward the water. Temperature contrasts between land and water are generally much smaller at night, hence land breezes are usually weaker than their daytime counterpart, the sea breeze. In regions where greater nighttime temperature contrasts exist, stronger land breezes occur over the water, off the coast.

They are not usually noticed much on shore, but are frequently observed by ships in coastal waters.

Mountain and Valley Breezes

[5] Mountain and valley breezes develop along mountain slopes. During the day, sunlight warms the valley walls, which in turn warm the air in contact with them. The heated air, being less dense than the air of the same altitude above the valley, rises as a gentle upslope wind known as a valley breeze. At night, the flow reverses. The mountain slopes cool quickly, chilling the air in contact with them. The cooler, more dense air glides downslope into the valley, providing a mountain breeze. (Because gravity is the force that directs these winds downhill, they are also referred to as *gravity winds,* or *drainage winds.*) This daily cycle of wind flow is best developed in clear, summer weather when prevailing winds are light.

[6] When the upslope valley winds are well developed and have sufficient moisture, they can reveal themselves as building cumulus clouds above mountain summits. Since valley breezes usually reach their maximum strength in the early afternoon, cloudiness, showers, and even thunderstorms are common over mountains during the warmest part of the day—a fact well known to climbers, hikers, and seasoned mountain picnickers.

Source: (1993). *Essentials of meteorology: An invitation to the atmosphere* (pp. 160–167). St. Paul, MN: West Publishing.

TASK 7: Look over the figures below. Scan the reading passage and determine which paragraph best describes each figure. Write the paragraph numbers in the spaces provided next to the illustrations and appropriately label the cool and warm areas.

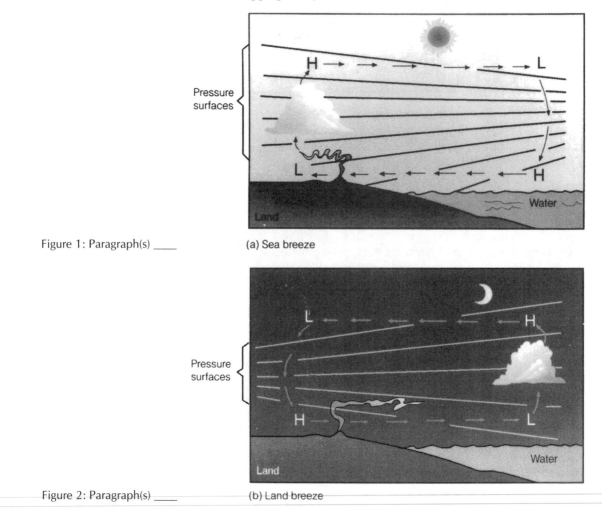

Figure 1: Paragraph(s) _____   (a) Sea breeze

Figure 2: Paragraph(s) _____   (b) Land breeze

Targeting Grammar: Subject-Verb Agreement with Present Tense Verbs

Many of the readings in this unit describe physical phenomena. Like many scientific texts, these descriptions use present tense verbs because they express general truths about our physical environment.

The subject of a sentence must agree with the verb in person (first, second, third) and in number (singular or plural). Remember that the third person singular requires an -*s* at the end of the verb.

THIRD PERSON	VERB	
Surface air	flow**s**	southward.
The land	heat**s**	more quickly.

Often the subject is separated from the verb by other sentence elements. In such sentences, first locate the verb, then the *head noun*, or main noun, which is the subject.

The air	above the land	becomes	cooler.
(head noun)	(modifier phrase)	(verb)	

One useful strategy for finding the head noun is to bracket [ ] phrases and clauses that come after and modify nouns.

The same **type** [of breeze] [that develops along the shore of a large lake] **is called** a lake breeze.
(head noun)   (verb)

When the subject is *there*, look for the "logical subject," which follows the verb.

There	**is**	a freezing	**wind**	from Siberia.
	(verb: singular)		(logical subject: singular)	

There	**are**	freezing	**winds**	from Siberia.
	(verb: plural)		(logical subject: plural)	

TASK 8: The sentences on the next page are taken or adapted from the readings in this unit. For each, do the following:

1. Find the main verb and underline it.
2. Put brackets around subject modifiers to identify the head noun of the subject.
3. Circle the head noun and state whether it is singular or plural.
4. Then check to see if the verb agrees with the head noun.

If there is a subject-verb agreement error, correct it. The first one has been done for you as an example.

1. The (mistral,) [a living force], <u>blow</u> grit in your face and perspective in your vision.
   Explanation: <u>Head noun: **mistral** = singular; verb: **blow** = plural; verb does not agree</u>
   <u>with head noun.</u>
   Correction: <u>The mistral, a living force, blows grit in your face and perspective in</u>
   <u>your vision.</u>

2. A high pressure system over mountains and plateaus converge with a low pressure storm system over mountains to produce a mistral.

   Explanation: _____

   _____

   Correction: _____

   _____

3. A person born during a dead calm, according to a legendary Irish poem, is destined to be a fool.

   Explanation: _____

   _____

   Correction: _____

   _____

4. Eric Sloane, in *Folklore of American Weather*, compare the east wind to a "boring guest that hasn't enough sense to leave."

   Explanation: _____

   _____

   Correction: _____

   _____

5. The uneven heating rates of land and water causes mesoscale coastal winds.

   Explanation: _____

   _____

   Correction: _____

   _____

6. The temperature contrasts between land and water are typically much smaller at night.

   Explanation: _____

   _____

   Correction: _____

   _____

Understanding through Listening 1

VIDEO

Lecture: Introduction to Atmospheric Environments
Segment 2: Thermal Circulation Systems

Professor: Jeffrey Lew
Course: Atmospheric Sciences 3: Introduction to Atmospheric Environments
Text: *Essentials of Meteorology* by C. Donald Ahrens

Before listening to an academic lecture, successful students prepare by thinking about the topic and *predicting* what the professor will discuss. Students can predict the topic and themes of the upcoming lecture based on information from previous lectures, assigned readings, and from the professor's syllabus.

ACADEMIC STRATEGY:

PREDICTING THE CONTENTS OF A LECTURE

TASK 9: To predict the information contained in the lecture segment, focus on the academic reading passages in this chapter. Look over "Local Wind Systems" on pages 63–64 and list the types of thermal circulation systems in the blanks below.

_____

_____

_____

_____

_____

TASK 10: Before watching the next lecture segment, look over Professor Lew's lecture outline below (which covers the next two lecture segments you will be listening to). Using your background knowledge and the information in "Local Wind Systems," predict what Professor Lew might discuss in each segment of the lecture. Then compare your hypotheses with those of your classmates.

II. Thermal Circulations
   A. Physics
   B. Sea/Land, Mountain/Valley Breezes
   C. Monsoons

III. Dynamically Forced Circulations
   A. Physics
   B. Foehn-type Winds, Chinook, Santa Ana

TASK 11: After predicting the lecture content, listen to the lecture segment and fill in the main daytime and nighttime characteristics of sea/land and mountain/valley breezes.

	SEA/LAND BREEZES	MOUNTAIN/VALLEY BREEZES
DAYTIME		
NIGHTTIME		

UNDERSTANDING THROUGH READING 2

ACADEMIC STRATEGY:

SKIMMING AND SCANNING

Skimming means reading a text very quickly in order to get an overview of the entire passage. Good readers skim at approximately 800 words per minute. This rate is double or triple their normal reading speed. For example, most people skim the newspaper in the morning in order to decide which articles to read in depth. This strategy is part of the previewing process and helps the reader develop a sense of what the article is about. It also helps the reader make stronger connections between new information in the article and previous knowledge. To skim a text, do the following:

- As in previewing, read the first and last paragraphs as well as the first and last sentence of the other paragraphs.
- Pay attention to proper nouns, dates, headings, italics, and boldface type and other marked text features (e.g., numbered lists, bulleted items).
- Do not try to understand the entire text. A 50-percent comprehension rate is considered average.

Scanning a text means looking over the text quickly to locate specific details rather than reading the entire text. For example, people scan a telephone book to locate a phone number or scan a history text to locate a specific name or date. Good readers use this technique when they are in need of a specific piece of information. To scan a text, do the following:

- Know as specifically as possible what information you are scanning to find.
- Let your eyes run quickly, left to right, over the text, paragraph by paragraph. Don't stop to read whole sentences. Instead, look for key words and phrases.
- When you find the key words, either stop and read the surrounding text for more information, or mark the place in some way, or make a mental note of having spotted the key words.

One important difference between skimming and scanning is that in skimming, readers do not have a predetermined goal other than acquiring a general overview of the text. In scanning, on the other hand, readers know specifically what information they want to locate.

TASK 12: Look over the information in the grid below. Then scan "Extreme Temperature Winds" (starting below) to locate the same information. Match the descriptions of wind types on the left with the natural phenomena on the right. Put the correct letter in the first column. Then write the number of the paragraph where this information is located next to the description. The first one has been done for you.

	DESCRIPTION/DETAILS	NATURAL PHENOMENA
_c_	1. downslope winds much stronger than mountain breezes (¶ _1_)	a. extreme temperature variation
___	2. polar invasion of cold air from Russia (¶ ___)	b. compressional heating
___	3. cold wind descending into the Rhône Valley of France (¶ ___)	c. katabatic winds
___	4. extensive damage such as toppled trees and a human fatality (¶ ___)	d. foehn winds
___	5. warm dry wind on the eastern slope of the Rocky Mountains (¶ ___)	e. effects of warm dry winds
___	6. warm dry wind in the Alps (¶ ___)	f. bora winds
___	7. main source of warm air for a chinook wind (¶ ___)	g. ferocious downslope wind
___	8. adverse human behavior, such as irritability and depression (¶ ___)	h. mistral winds
___	9. two-minute 49° temperature change recorded in South Dakota (¶ ___)	i. chinook winds

TASK 13: Now read the excerpt. Notice whether your comprehension is improved after doing the previous scanning exercise.

EXTREME TEMPERATURE WINDS

C. Donald Ahrens

Katabatic Winds

[1]   Although any downslope wind is technically a katabatic wind, the name is usually reserved for downslope winds that are much stronger than mountain breezes. Katabatic (or fall) winds can rush down elevated slopes at hurricane speeds, but most are not that intense and many are on the order of 10 knots or less.

[2]   The ideal setting for a katabatic wind is an elevated plateau surrounded by mountains, with an opening that slopes rapidly downhill. When winter snows accumulate on the plateau, the overlying air grows extremely cold. Along the edge of the plateau the cold, dense air begins to descend through gaps and saddles in the hills, usually as a gentle or moderate cold breeze. If the breeze, however, is confined to a narrow canyon or channel, the flow of air can increase, often destructively, as cold air rushes downslope like water flowing over a fall.

[3]   Katabatic winds are observed in various regions of the world. For example, along the northern Adriatic coast in Yugoslavia, a polar invasion of cold air from Russia descends the slopes from a high plateau and reaches the lowlands as the *bora*—a cold, gusty, northeasterly wind with speeds sometimes in excess of 100 knots. A similar, but often less violent, cold wind known as the *mistral* descends the western mountains into the Rhone Valley of France, and then out over the Mediterranean Sea. It frequently causes frost damage to exposed vineyards and makes people bundle up in the otherwise mild climate along the Riviera. Strong, cold katabatic winds also blow downslope off the icecaps in Greenland and Antarctica occasionally, with speeds greater than 100 knots.

[4]   In North America, when cold air accumulates over the Columbia plateau, it may flow westward through the Columbia River Gorge as a strong, gusty, and sometimes violent wind. Even though the sinking air warms by compression, it is so cold to begin with that it reaches the ocean side of the Cascade Mountains much colder than the marine air it replaces. The *Columbia Gorge wind* is often the harbinger of a prolonged cold spell.

[5]   Strong downslope katabatic-type winds funneled through a mountain canyon can do extensive damage. For example, during January, 1984, a ferocious downslope wind blew through Yosemite National Park with speeds estimated at 100 knots. The wind toppled trees and caused a fatality when a tree fell on a park employee sleeping in a tent.

Chinook (Foehn) Winds

[6]   The chinook wind is a warm, dry wind that descends the eastern slope of the Rocky Mountains. The region of the chinook is rather narrow and extends from northeastern New Mexico northward into Canada. Similar winds occur along the leeward slopes of mountains in other regions of the world. In the Alps, for example, such a wind is called a *foehn*. When these winds move through an area, the temperature rises sharply, sometimes over 20°C (36°F) in one hour, and a corresponding sharp drop in the relative humidity occurs, occasionally to less than 5 percent.

[7]   Chinooks occur when strong westerly winds aloft flow over a north-south-trending mountain range, such as the Rockies and Cascades. Such conditions can produce a trough of low pressure on the mountain's eastern side, a trough that tends to force the air downslope. As the air descends, it is compressed and warms. So the main source of warmth for a chinook is *compressional heating,* as potentially warmer (and drier) air is brought down from aloft.

[8]   When clouds and precipitation occur on the mountain's windward side, they can enhance the chinook. For example, as the cloud forms on the windward side of the mountain, the conversion of latent heat to sensible heat supplements the compressional heating on the leeward side. This phenomenon makes the descending air at the base of the mountain on the leeward side warmer than it was before it started its upward journey on the windward side. The air is also drier, since much of its moisture was removed as precipitation on the windward side.

[9]   Along the front range of the Rockies, a bank of clouds forming over the mountains is a telltale sign of an impending chinook. This *chinook wall* cloud usually remains stationary as air rises, condenses, and then rapidly descends the leeward slopes, often causing strong winds in foothill communities.

Snow Eaters and Rapid Temperature Changes

[10]   Chinooks are thirsty winds. As they move over a heavy snow cover, they can melt and evaporate a foot of snow in less than a day. This has led to some tall tales about these so-called "snow eaters." Canadian folklore has it that a sled-driving traveler once tried to outrun a chinook. During the entire ordeal his front runners were in snow while his back runners were on bare soil.

[11]   Actually, the chinook is important economically. It not only brings relief from the winter cold, but it uncovers prairie grass, so that livestock can graze on the open range. Also, these warm winds have kept railroad tracks clear of snow, so that trains can keep running. On the other hand, the drying effect of a chinook can create an extreme fire hazard. And when a chinook follows spring planting, the seeds may die in the parched soil. Along with the dry air comes a buildup of static electricity, making a simple handshake a shocking experience. These warm, dry winds have sometimes adversely affected human behavior. During periods of chinook winds some people feel irritable and depressed and others become ill. The exact reason for this phenomenon is not clearly understood.

[12]   Chinook winds have been associated with rapid temperature changes. A shallow layer of extremely cold air can move southward out of Canada and rest against the Rocky Mountains. In the cold air, temperatures are near 5°F, while just a short distance up the mountain a warm chinook wind raises the air temperature to 45°F. The cold air behaves just as any fluid, and, in some cases, atmospheric conditions may cause the air to move up and down much like water does when a bowl is rocked back and forth. This can cause extreme temperature variations for cities located at the base of the hills along the periphery of the cold air–warm air boundary, as they are alternately in and then out of the cold air. Such a situation is held to be responsible for the unbelievable two-minute temperature change of 49° recorded at Spearfish, South Dakota, on January 22, 1943.

Source: (1993). *Essentials of meteorology: An invitation to the atmosphere* (pp. 160–167). St. Paul, MN: West Publishing.

Targeting Vocabulary: Word Families

Often new vocabulary is acquired in isolation, one word at a time. A more productive way to learn new vocabulary for academic reading and writing is to learn words in "families." In other words, when learning a new verb, the noun and adjective forms of that verb should be learned at the same time. Here is an example of a word family:

VERB	NOUN	ADJECTIVE	ADVERB
circulate	circulation	circulated/circulating*	none**

* The -ed and -ing adjective endings are the past and present participle forms of the verb. Participles can act as adjectives. The person, place, or thing that this kind of adjective modifies receives the action or quality that the adjective describes. For example, in the sentence *"People can be irritated by chinook winds,"* the participle *irritated* modifies *people*.

** Note that not all words have an adverbial form.

TASK 14: The following words are from the readings in this unit. Using a dictionary, look up the meaning of each word. Provide the missing members of each word family. The first one has been done for you.

VERB	NOUN	ADJECTIVE	ADVERB
to accumulate	accumulation	accumulative	accumulatively
		compressional	
to condense			
		descending	
			destructively
	elevation		
	excess		
to evaporate			
	invasion		
		irritable	
		observant	

Targeting Grammar: Adverbs of Manner, Place, and Direction

Adverbs of manner describe how something is done or happens. Many of these adverbs end in *–ly*:

destructively	slowly
quickly	swiftly
sharply	suddenly

Adverbs of manner can function as prepositional phrases:

in a destructive manner
with great speed

Adverbs of place and *direction* indicate where an event occurs. Prepositional phrases can also function as adverbs of place and direction:

SINGLE WORDS		PREPOSITIONAL PHRASES	
PLACE	**DIRECTION**	**PLACE**	**DIRECTION**
above	north	from a high plateau	toward the east
below	west	along the leeward slope	from the west
here	northeast	above a river	through a mountain pass
there	downslope	in a valley	along the river

Usually adverbs of manner, place, and direction are placed after the verb:

The temperature may **rise**   **sharply** when a foehn wind moves through an area.
        (verb)   (manner)

Similar winds **occur**   **along the leeward slopes of mountains** in other regions of the world.
      (verb)   (place)

A ferocious downslope wind **blew**   **through Yosemite National Park.**
          (verb)   (place)

TASK 15: The sentences below are taken from or adapted from readings in this unit. For each sentence do the following:

1. Circle adverbs and prepositional phrases of manner, place, and direction.
2. Underline the verb that each adverb or phrase modifies.
3. Answer these questions on the lines provided:

   • Does each adverb or phrase describe manner, place, or direction?

   • Do the positions of the adverbs follow the general rule of placement?

   • In sentences that have more than one adverb or phrase, in what order do the different kinds appear?

The first one has been done as an example.

1. Cypresses, the most exposed of trees, <u>flexed</u> (acutely) (in the line of the wind.)

<u>acutely=adverb of manner; in the line of the wind=adverb of direction</u>

<u>The adverb of manner comes before the adverb of direction.</u>

2. The wind raged across the hill above, tearing into freshly bloomed cascades of yellow broom so that the color writhed.

_____

_____

3. The dense air glides downslope into the valley, providing a mountain breeze.

_____

_____

4. Katabatic winds can rush down elevated slopes at hurricane speeds.

_____

_____

5. Strong, cold katabatic winds also blow downslope off the icecaps in Greenland and Antarctica occasionally, with speeds greater than 100 knots.

_____

_____

UNDERSTANDING THROUGH LISTENING 2

VIDEO

Lecture: Introduction to Atmospheric Environments
Segment 3: Foehn and Chinook Winds

Professor: Jeffrey Lew
Course: Atmospheric Sciences 3: Introduction to Atmospheric Environments
Text: _Essentials of Meteorology_ by C. Donald Ahrens

TASK 16: Before viewing the next segment of the lecture by Professor Lew, look over the map of the Western United States below. Note the location of the states and the geographical features.

TASK 17: These two diagrams illustrate information that Professor Lew will explain in his lecture. With a partner, take turns explaining the diagrams, using information from the reading "Extreme Temperature Winds."

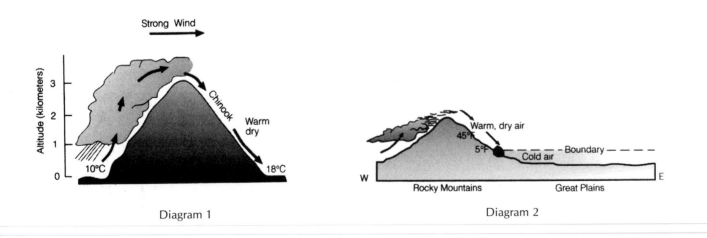

Diagram 1

Diagram 2

TASK 18: As you watch the lecture, number in sequence the geographical locations that Professor Lew mentions. Then locate these places on the map in Task 16. You may need to watch the lecture more than once. The first one has been done for you.

_____ Colorado   _____ New Mexico

_____ Montana   __1__ Rocky Mountains

_____ Pacific   _____ Kansas

_____ Wyoming   _____ Oklahoma

_____ Idaho   _____ Utah

TASK 19: View the lecture again. Provide the information relevant to the key terms listed in the grid below. The first one has been completed as an example.

KEY TERM	RELEVANT INFORMATION
foehn-type wind	phenomenon where the air apparently warms up while going over a mountain, even though it ends up at the same altitude on the other side
windward side of the Rockies	
winter wind direction	
50° to 60°	
3,000 to 7,000 ft.	
chinook	

Integrating Perspectives

APPLYING THE CONCEPTS

TASK 20: Examine the information in the grid below. Which ideas were presented in the lectures? Which appeared in the reading passages? Put a check mark in the appropriate column. Note that some concepts will have appeared in both sources.

INFORMATION	LECTURE	READING
1. Explanation of land/sea thermal circulations	√	√
2. Explanation of day/night thermal circulations		
3. Occurrence of foehn winds in the Alps		
4. Canadian folktale dealing with chinook winds		
5. Occurrence of thunderstorms over mountains		
6. Occurrence of katabatic winds in Yosemite National Park		
7. Explanation of mountain/valley thermal circulations		
8. Evaporation rate of snow during chinook winds		
9. Existence of cold mistral winds in Southern France		

TASK 21: Examine the completed grid above and compare the information from the lecture with the concepts from the reading. What information is duplicated? What information is found in only one source? Why is it important to note this difference?

ANALYZING THROUGH DISCUSSION

Students often study with a partner or form study groups to prepare for quizzes and examinations. Each person in the study group may take responsibility for a different topic or section of the material and contribute this information to the group's study session. This is an efficient study strategy because it allows individuals to specialize in a particular area and then teach this information to others. Another method of group study is for each person to prepare a synthesis of the material and then for group members to compare their syntheses, noting gaps in information and resolving contradictions in the information. Here are some tips for effective study groups:

ACADEMIC STRATEGY:

STUDYING WITH A PARTNER

- Share notes and compare major points recorded.
- Quiz each other on key terms and concepts.
- Note materials that appear in both the readings and the lectures. This information is important and will likely be covered on an exam.
- Predict the questions that the instructor will ask, and prepare sample answers.

TASK 22: Imagine that Professor Lew has scheduled a test on the readings and lecture segments in this unit so far. With a partner or a small group, predict three terms that you might need to define and three short-answer essay questions that Professor Lew might include. Present these items and your answers to your classmates.

EVALUATING THROUGH WRITING

TASK 23: On a separate paper, write a brief paragraph about thermal circulations, synthesizing the information from the lectures and the readings.

EXPANSION:

HOT WINDS

The last two chapters have explored local winds and the physics of winds. Many people think that winds can have an effect on people's emotions and mental states. This chapter focuses on warm wind systems and the interplay between individuals and their environment.

Exploring the Concepts

EXPLORING THROUGH VISUAL IMAGES

TASK 1: Read the cartoon and, in small groups, discuss what the cartoonist is trying to convey about the interplay between people and natural forces, such as wind systems.

Calvin and Hobbes   by Bill Watterson

EXPLORING THROUGH DISCUSSION

Winds have both positive and negative effects. In this chapter, you will learn about some of the negative effects that winds have—on both humans and their physical environment.

Task 2: With a partner or in a small group, use the cluster diagram to brainstorm the negative effects that winds can have on humans and their environment.

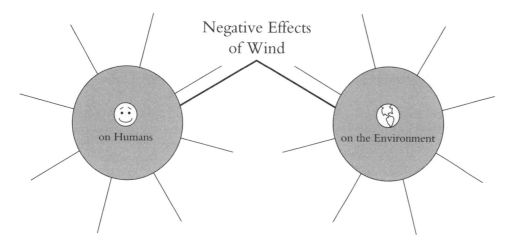

Task 3: This chapter deals specifically with hot wind systems. Predict which of the negative effects you listed above relate to this kind of wind system. Share this information with the rest of the class.

EXPLORING THROUGH WRITING

Task 4: Weather systems, and winds in particular, can affect how people feel both physically and mentally. Write a journal entry describing a time in your life when you were strongly influenced by winds or weather. Share this journal entry with your classmates.

Working with Sources

UNDERSTANDING THROUGH READING 1

A well-known example of a hot wind is the Santa Ana wind in Southern California. These hot winds are famous for the extensive fire damage they cause as well as their psychological effects on the inhabitants of the region.

Task 5: Look at the partial map of the United States below. This map shows weather conditions for January 17, 1976, when a "Santa Ana condition" was in effect in Southern California. Working with your classmates, predict why there are temperature differences across the states, and what effect these might have on local wind systems.

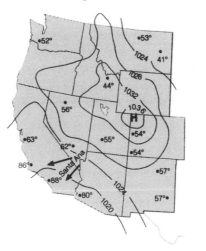

Targeting Vocabulary: Finding Synonyms or Paraphrases

The next passage deals with the formation of hot winds in desert regions—how they originate, blow, and affect the region in which they are found. The passage contains many verbs that describe the movement of hot winds.

TASK 6: Scan the passage to find each verb listed below. Then write the paragraph number in the column and give a synonym or paraphrase. Refer to a dictionary if necessary.

WORD	PARAGRAPH	SYNONYM OR PARAPHRASE
1. blow	1	to move with force
2. descend		
3. funnel		
4. spread		
5. develop		
6. force		
7. dry out		
8. rush		
9. originate		
10. lift		
11. damage		
12. destroy		
13. form		
14. deflect		
15. last		

TASK 7: The excerpt below describes the formation of Santa Ana winds and other desert winds. As you read, highlight the sequence of events in this process for each type of wind.

SANTA ANA WINDS

C. Donald Ahrens

[1]   A warm, dry wind that blows from the east or northeast into Southern California is the Santa Ana wind. As the air descends from the elevated desert plateau, it funnels through mountain canyons in the San Gabriel and San Bernardino Mountains, finally spreading over the Los Angeles Basin and San Fernando Valley. The wind often blows with exceptional speed in the Santa Ana Canyon (the canyon from which it derives its name).

[2]   These warm, dry winds develop as a region of high pressure builds over the Great Basin. The clockwise circulation around the anticyclone forces air downslope from the high plateau. Thus, *compressional heating* provides the primary source of warming. The air is dry, since it originated in the desert, and it dries out even more as it is heated.

[3]   As the wind rushes through canyon passes, it lifts dust and sand and dries out vegetation. This sets the stage for serious brush fires, especially in autumn, when chaparral-covered hills are already parched from the dry summer. One such fire in November of 1961—

the infamous Bel Air fire—burned for three days, destroying 484 homes and causing over $25 million in damage. During October, 1977, Santa Ana-driven flames scorched 25,000 acres along a 10-mile-wide swath across the Santa Monica Mountains, destroying 91 homes collectively valued at several million dollars. Four hundred miles to the north in Oakland, California, a ferocious Santa Ana-type wind was responsible for the disastrous Oakland hills fire during October, 1991, that damaged or destroyed over 3000 dwellings and took 25 lives. With the protective vegetation cover removed, the land is ripe for erosion, as winter rains wash away topsoil and, in some areas, create serious mudslides. The adverse effects of a wind-driven Santa Ana fire may be felt throughout the year.

Desert Winds

[4] Local winds form in deserts, too. Dust storms form in dry regions, where strong winds are able to lift and fill the air with particles of fine dust. In desert areas where loose sand is more prevalent, sandstorms develop, as high winds enhanced by surface heating rapidly carry sand particles close to the ground. A spectacular example of a storm composed of dust or sand is the *haboob* (from Arabic *hebbe:* blown). The haboob forms as cold downdrafts along the leading edge of a thunderstorm lift dust or sand into a huge, tumbling dark cloud that may extend horizontally for over a hundred miles and rise vertically to the base of the thunderstorm. Spinning whirlwinds of dust frequently form along the turbulent cold air boundary, giving rise to sightings of huge *dust devils* and even tornadoes. Haboobs are most common in the African Sudan (where about twenty-four occur each year) and in the desert southwest of the United States, especially in southern Arizona.

[5] The spinning vortices so commonly seen on hot days in dry areas are called whirlwinds, or dust devils. (In Australia, the Aboriginal word *willy-willy* is used to refer to a dust devil.) Generally, dust devils form on clear, hot days, as warm air rises above a heated surface. Wind, often deflected by small topographic barriers, flows into this region, rotating the rising air. Depending on the nature of the topographic feature, the spin of a dust devil around its central eye may be cyclonic or anticyclonic, and both directions occur with about equal frequency.

[6] Having diameters of only a few meters and heights of less than 100 meters (300 feet), most dust devils are small and last only a short time. There are, however, some dust devils of sizable dimension, extending upward from the surface for many hundreds of meters. Such whirlwinds are capable of considerable damage; winds exceeding 75 knots may overturn mobile homes and tear the roofs off buildings. Fortunately, the majority of dust devils are small.

Source: (1993). *Essentials of meteorology: An invitation to the atmosphere* (pp. 160–167). St. Paul, MN: West Publishing.

Targeting Grammar: Nonrestrictive Relative Clauses Indicating Location

A type of dependent clause commonly used to provide detail is the *nonrestrictive relative clause indicating location*. These clauses are introduced by the relative clause marker *where*. Note that the locational clause directly follows the noun it modifies and is always set off by a comma. Look at the sentences below:

Dust storms form in the Mojave Desert, **where** strong winds are able to lift and fill the air with particles of fine dust.

In southern Arizona, **where** loose sand is more prevalent, sandstorms often develop.

Task 8: Match the items in each column, taken from the reading passage "Santa Ana Winds." Then use the matched information to write a sentence using a locational clause. Be sure to vary the position of the clauses within the sentences. The first one has been done for you.

	LOCATION	ADDITIONAL INFORMATION
_d_	1. African Sudan	a. region of high pressure
	2. Australia	b. wind funnels through canyons
	3. Bel Air	c. 25 lives were lost
	4. Great Basin	d. haboob winds are common
	5. Oakland	e. 484 homes were destroyed
	6. San Gabriel and San Bernardino Mountains	f. dust devils are called *willy-willies*

1. Haboobs are common in the African Sudan, where about 24 occur each year.

2. _____

_____

3. _____

_____

4. _____

_____

5. _____

_____

6. _____

_____

UNDERSTANDING THROUGH LISTENING

VIDEO

Lecture: Introduction to Atmospheric Environments
Segment 4: Santa Ana Winds

Professor: Jeffrey Lew
Course: Atmospheric Sciences 3: Introduction to Atmospheric Environments
Text: *Essentials of Meteorology* by C. Donald Ahrens

In this next lecture segment, Professor Lew explains the origins and effects of the Santa Ana winds.

TASK 9: Professor Lew mentions the geographical terms listed below. Watch the lecture and number the terms in the order that you hear them. Then locate each place on the map on page 74. Finally, in the right-hand column, indicate whether the term refers to a region, state, mountain range, or city. One example has been done for you.

ORDER	GEOGRAPHICAL TERM	REGION, STATE, MOUNTAIN RANGE, OR CITY?
____	Great Plains	
____	Idaho	
__1__	Los Angeles	*city*
____	Montana	
____	Nevada	
____	Riverside	
____	San Gabriel	
____	Santa Ana	
____	Southern California	
____	Tehachapi	
____	Utah	

TASK 10: Professor Lew provides a visual representation, looking south, of how Santa Ana winds originate and how they interact with the sea breezes. Watch the lecture a second time and complete the diagram below with the key information he provides. Then take turns explaining it to a partner.

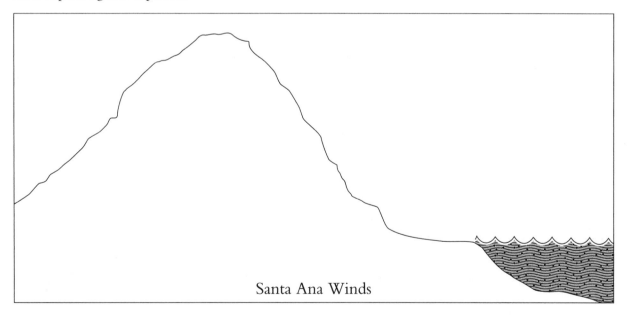

Santa Ana Winds

Targeting Grammar: Using Articles with Geographical Terms

In most cases, the choice of article for geographical and atmospheric terms is either *no article* (also referred to as the *zero article*) or the definite article *the*. Here are article usage rules for many of the geographical terms found in this unit.

1. Use the zero article in front of most cities, states or provinces, and countries:

CITIES	STATES/PROVINCES	COUNTRIES
New York	Colorado	Canada
Frankfurt	Manitoba	Egypt
Singapore	Queensland	Morocco

    a. Note that the zero article is used even when these categories are modified by adjectives of location such as *northern, eastern, central,* etc.

       south central Los Angeles, northern New Mexico, southern France

    b. Some exceptions to this rule are names of cities, states, or provinces, and countries that are modified by an *of*-phrase or the words *United* or *Union:*

       the city of Rome, **the** southern tip of Florida, **the** United Arab Emirates

2. Use *the* before proper nouns in these categories:

OCEANS	SEAS	RIVERS
the Pacific Ocean	the Mediterranean Sea	the Columbia River
the Atlantic Ocean	the Baltic Sea	the Rhône River

REGIONS	DESERTS	MOUNTAIN RANGES
the Midi	the Sahara	the Rocky Mountains
the Midwest	the Gobi Desert	the Alps

VALLEYS	PASSES	COASTAL AREAS
the Rhône Valley	the Cajon Pass	the Adriatic coast
the San Fernando Valley	the Saint Bernard Pass	the Newfoundland shore

    a. Note that *the* is used even when these categories are modified by adjectives of location such as *northern, eastern, central,* etc.

       the central Sahara, **the** northeastern Atlantic coast, **the** lower Mississippi valley

    b. Note also that plural nouns indicating geographical location take *the*:

       the Great Plains, **the** Seychelles, **the** Florida Keys

3. Article usage with the names of winds depends on the context:
  a. Use *the* before the name of a wind when defining or describing it:

  The mistral is a wind that blows from the north through the Rhône Valley.
  The haboob is a Sudan dust storm that is often followed by rain.

  b. Use *a* before the name of a wind when it is first mentioned in a narrative context:

  A mistral raced through the valley.
  A sandstorm started just as we set out on our hike.

  c. With plural names of winds, both *the* and the zero article are possible:

  (The) Chinook winds derive their warmth from compressional heating.
    (The zero article is frequently used when generalizing about the properties of a wind.)

  The chinook winds roared through the valley this morning.
    (When talking about a specific case of a plural wind, the tendency is to use *the*.)

TASK 11: Each of the following phrases is a headline for a newspaper weather story. Since headlines are abbreviated messages, they usually leave out articles. Transform each headline into a grammatically correct sentence, adding articles and making other necessary changes. (Put verbs in the progressive *-ing* form if you think the event is happening now; use present perfect tense if you think the event was recently completed.) Remember that all singular count nouns need articles. The first one has been done as an example.

1. SANTA ANAS MOVE TOWARD PACIFIC OCEAN

The Santa Anas are moving toward the Pacific Ocean. (still happening)

2. MISTRAL DESCENDS INTO RHÔNE VALLEY

_____

3. KATABATIC WINDS SWEEP THROUGH CASCADE MOUNTAINS

_____

4. FIRES DRIVEN BY SANTA ANAS BURN 25,000 ACRES

_____

5. MISTRAL WINDS SPLINTER HOUSES IN SOUTHERN FRANCE

_____

6. DUST DEVIL WIND TEARS ROOFS OFF HOUSES IN EASTERN PART OF AUSTRALIA

_____

7. HABOOB WREAKS HAVOC IN DESERT TOWN IN SOUTHERN ARIZONA

_____

8. CHINOOK WARMS EASTERN SLOPE OF ROCKIES

_____

UNDERSTANDING THROUGH READING 2

The following reading, taken from the *Los Angeles Times Magazine,* is about how winds can worsen a natural disaster.

TASK 12: Before reading the passage, scan it to locate the verbs the author uses to describe wind and fire. Write the verbs in the chart below. Then read the passage.

WINDS	FIRES
sweep	putter

THE WISE MAN OF THE MOUNTAINS

Patrick Goldstein

[1]   Wind is what makes a fire deadly. When the Santa Anas sweep in from the northeast, they blow the dusty desert air through the canyons and, after a couple of days, out to the Pacific, knocking the waves flat. Gary Nelson, a Los Angeles County assistant fire chief, has seen winds whip through canyons at a hurricane-like 80-to-100 m.p.h. In 1982, a fire started on the western side of the San Fernando Valley, burned over the hills, jumped the Ventura Freeway and raced all the way to the ocean.

[2]   Under normal conditions, a fire will putter along at about a quarter of a mile to a half a mile an hour. At that speed, most blazes can be brought under control with water drops from helicopters and air tankers. But if most fires rumble along like a dump truck, a Santa Ana-driven blaze races through the hills like a Ferrari, moving at 2 or 3, sometimes 4 m.p.h. It doesn't sound like much until you've been out on the line, watching a fire eat up ground as fast as a sprinter running a 440.

[3]   "When a Santa Ana is blowing," he says, driving along the path of the Old Topanga fire, "it doesn't matter about uphill or downhill, you're not gonna stop the fire."

[4]   Once a wind-driven fire starts, it simply can't be stopped. Barely 90 minutes after the Old Topanga fire had started, Nelson watched the wind-buffeted blaze race south out of the Calabasas Highlands. He knew exactly where it would be later that afternoon. "There was no sense trying to stop the fire," he recalls. "It was going to go to the ocean."

[5]   The best defense against such an overwhelming adversary: Fire Guy humor. "We're famous for stopping all our fires at the Pacific Ocean," Nelson says. "We've never had one go any further. We'd be in big trouble if we were in Colorado, wouldn't we?"

Source: (1995, February). *Los Angeles Times Magazine,* 23–24.

ⓔ Targeting Vocabulary: Similes

In "The Wise Man of the Mountains," Goldstein uses similes to describe the speed of fires driven by wind. A *simile* is a figure of speech that compares one thing to another using *like* or *as*. Look at the following sentences and note how this literary device is structured.

> The **Santa Anas,** winds off the mountains of California, are **as warm as an oven.**
> The **mistral** uprooted trees **like a bulldozer gone wild.**

TASK 13: Scan "The Wise Man of the Mountains" again, locating the similes that describe how quickly the fire was moving. List three of the similes in the space provided below.

1. _____

2. _____

3. _____

TASK 14: In your journal, describe an event or disaster that was caused by wind. Use similes to enrich the description.

TASK 15: Write a paragraph to be added to "The Wise Man of the Mountains" explaining scientifically how Santa Ana winds form. Use the information from Professor Lew's lecture and "Santa Ana Winds." Decide where to locate this paragraph in "The Wise Man of the Mountains." Remember to use the present tense for scientific explanation.

Integrating Perspectives

EVALUATING THROUGH LITERATURE

The following essay describes the effects of Santa Ana winds on the residents of Southern California.

TASK 16: Use a highlighter pen to identify the passages that describe the geographical effects and the physical/emotional effects of the Santa Ana winds.

LOS ANGELES NOTEBOOK

Joan Didion

[1]   There is something uneasy in the Los Angeles air this afternoon, some unnatural stillness, some tension. What it means is that tonight a Santa Ana will begin to blow, a hot wind from the northeast whining down through the Cajon and San Gorgonio Passes, blowing up sandstorms out along Route 66, drying the hills and the nerves to the flash point. For a few days now we will see smoke back in the canyons, and hear sirens in the night. I have neither heard nor read that a Santa Ana is due, but I know it, and almost everyone I have seen today knows it too. We know it because we feel it. The baby frets. The maid sulks. I rekindle a waning argument with the telephone company, then cut my losses and lie down, given over to whatever it is in the air. To live with the Santa Ana is to accept, consciously or unconsciously, a deeply mechanistic view of human behavior.

[2]   I recall being told, when I first moved to Los Angeles and was living on an isolated beach, that the Indians would throw themselves into the sea when the bad wind blew. I could see why. The Pacific turned ominously glossy during a Santa Ana period, and one woke in the night troubled not only by the peacocks screaming in the olive trees but by the eerie absence of

surf. The heat was surreal. The sky had a yellow cast, the kind of light sometimes called "earthquake weather." My only neighbor would not come out of her house for days, and there were no lights at night, and her husband roamed the place with a machete. One day he would tell me that he had heard a trespasser, the next a rattlesnake.

[3]   "On nights like that," Raymond Chandler once wrote about the Santa Ana, "every booze party ends in a fight. Meek little wives feel the edge of the carving knife and study their husbands' necks. Anything can happen." That was the kind of wind it was. I did not know then that there was any basis for the effect it had on all of us, but it turns out to be another of those cases in which science bears out folk wisdom. The Santa Ana, which is named for one of the canyons it rushes through, is a *foehn* wind, like the *foehn* of Austria and Switzerland and the *hamsin* of Israel. There are a number of persistent malevolent winds, perhaps the best known of which are the mistral of France and the Mediterranean sirocco, but a *foehn* wind has distinct characteristics: it occurs on the leeward slope of a mountain range and, although the air begins as a cold mass, it is warmed as it comes down the mountain and appears finally as a hot dry wind. Whenever and wherever a *foehn* blows, doctors hear about headaches and nausea and allergies, about "nervousness," about "depression." In Los Angeles some teachers do not attempt to conduct formal classes during a Santa Ana, because the children become unmanageable. In Switzerland the suicide rate goes up during the *foehn*, and in the courts of some Swiss cantons the wind is considered a mitigating circumstance for crime. Surgeons are said to watch the wind, because blood does not clot normally during a *foehn*. A few years ago an Israeli physicist discovered that not only during such winds, but for the ten or twelve hours which precede them, the air carries an unusually high ratio of positive to negative ions. No one seems to know exactly why that should be; some talk about friction and others suggest solar disturbances. In any case the positive ions are there, and what an excess of positive ions does, in the simplest terms, is make people unhappy. One cannot get much more mechanistic than that.

[4]   Easterners commonly complain that there is no "weather" at all in Southern California, that the days and the seasons slip by relentlessly, numbingly bland. That is quite misleading. In fact the climate is characterized by infrequent but violent extremes: two periods of torrential subtropical rains which continue for weeks and wash out the hills and send subdivisions sliding toward the sea; about twenty scattered days a year of the Santa Ana,

which, with its incendiary dryness, invariably means fire. At the first prediction of a Santa Ana, the Forest Service flies men and equipment from Northern California into the southern forests, and the Los Angeles Fire Department cancels its ordinary non-fire fighting routines. The Santa Ana caused Malibu to burn the way it did in 1956, and Bel Air in 1961, and Santa Barbara in 1964. In the winter of 1966–67 eleven men were killed fighting a Santa Ana fire that spread through the San Gabriel Mountains.

[5]   Just to watch the front-page news out of Los Angeles during a Santa Ana is to get very close to what it is about the place. The longest single Santa Ana period in recent years was in 1957, and it lasted not the usual three or four days but fourteen days, from November 21 until December 4. On the first day 25,000 acres of the San Gabriel Mountains were burning, with gusts reaching 100 miles an hour. In town, the wind reached Force 12, or hurricane force, on the Beaufort Scale; oil derricks were toppled and people ordered off the downtown streets to avoid injury from flying objects. On November 22 the fire in the San Gabriels was out of control. On November 24 six people were killed in automobile accidents, and by the end of the week the Los Angeles *Times* was keeping a box score of traffic deaths. On November 26 a prominent Pasadena attorney, depressed about money, shot and killed his wife, their two sons, and himself. On November 27 a South Gate divorcee, twenty-two, was murdered and thrown from a moving car. On November 30 the San Gabriel fire was still out of control, and the wind in town was blowing eighty miles an hour. On the first day of December four people died violently, and on the third the wind began to break.

[6]   It is hard for people who have not lived in Los Angeles to realize how radically the Santa Ana figures in the local imagination. The city burning is Los Angeles's deepest image of itself: Nathanael West perceived that, in *The Day of the Locust*; and at the time of the 1965 Watts riots what struck the imagination most indelibly were the fires. For days one could drive to the Harbor Freeway and see the city on fire, just as we had always known it would be in the end. Los Angeles weather is the weather of catastrophe, of apocalypse, and, just as the reliably long and bitter winters of New England determine the way life is lived there, so the violence and the unpredictability of the Santa Ana affect the entire quality of life in Los Angeles, accentuate its impermanence, its unreliability. The wind shows us how close to the edge we are.

Source: (1968). *Slouching towards Bethlehem* (pp. 217–221). New York: Dell Publishing.

TASK 17: Study the sections of the text that you highlighted in Task 16 and compare them in small groups. Note that the geographical effects and the effects on people fall into two categories: before and during the winds. Fill in the chart below, being sure to add the paragraph number where the information can be found. An example has been completed for you.

GEOGRAPHICAL EFFECTS	
BEFORE	**DURING**
	The Pacific turned ominously glossy during a Santa Ana period. (¶2)

EFFECTS ON HUMANS	
BEFORE	**DURING**
The baby frets. The maid sulks. (¶1)	

TASK 18: Good writers often weave together evidence from a variety of sources to enrich their writing and make it more effective. For example, Joan Didion juxtaposes scientific fact, personal anecdotes, vivid description, news items, and references to literature in her piece "Los Angeles Notebook." To analyze how effectively Didion does this, scan the reading to find these pieces of evidence. Then write the paragraph numbers that relate to each category in the chart below. The first one is done for you as an example.

	SCIENTIFIC FACT	PERSONAL ANECDOTE	VIVID DESCRIPTION	NEWS ITEM	REFERENCES TO LITERATURE
¶ No.	3, 4, and 5				

APPLYING THE CONCEPTS

TASK 19: In "Santa Ana Winds," "The Wise Man of the Mountains," and "Los Angeles Notebook," Santa Ana winds are described from three perspectives: those of a scientist, a firefighter, and a writer. Scan the three readings in order to fill in the chart below.

PERSPECTIVES	PHYSICAL EFFECTS	PSYCHOLOGICAL EFFECTS
The scientist		
The firefighter		
The writer		

TASK 20: What are the similarities and differences concerning the effects of Santa Ana winds as described from these three perspectives? What generalizations can you make about this information?

EVALUATING THROUGH WRITING

This unit has examined winds from the perspectives of personal experience, scientific explanation, news events, folklore, and literature. The underlying theme of the readings and lecture segments has been the effects of different winds on the lives of human beings.

TASK 21: Select one of the topics below and write an essay using personal experience and the knowledge gained from this unit. Study the Academic Strategy box on page 91 to learn about supporting a thesis. In your essay, make sure to provide a variety of support to strengthen your thesis.

1. In "Los Angeles Notebook," Joan Didion writes: ". . . but it turns out to be another of those cases in which science bears out folk wisdom." Support this statement by explaining how scientific data can be used to prove or disprove folk wisdom.

2. In "Relish the Rhône," Clive Irving writes: "Then came the mistral to remind us that Mother Nature can be a spoiler too." Support this statement by describing the physical effects of the weather on us and our environment.

3. In "Los Angeles Notebook," Joan Didion writes: "The wind shows us how close to the edge we are." Support this statement by discussing how the weather can cause personality and behavior changes.

TASK 20: To check your comprehension of the reading passage, decide if the following statements are true or false and write your answer on the line. Write the number of the paragraph(s) that support(s) your decision. The first one has been done for you.

False (¶ 2) 1. The Statue of Liberty was built to welcome immigrants to the United States.

_____ 2. Until recently historians tended to view immigrants as refugees fleeing an unhappy environment.

_____ 3. Both Lazarus and Handlin romanticized the immigrants to America.

_____ 4. During the late nineteenth century, many immigrants entered the United States illegally from Canada and Mexico.

_____ 5. An early view held that immigrants had to give up their cultural heritage in order to be successful in the New World.

_____ 6. Historians now believe that one's ethnicity, race, or religion determined one's immigration experience and reasons for emigrating.

Targeting Vocabulary: Connotation and Denotation

When writers select words, they must carefully consider the *denotation,* or dictionary meaning of the words they choose; they must also consider the *connotation,* or emotional impact of these same words. Many words have a positive or negative connotation in specific contexts, and these words reflect the author's tone, point of view, or opinion about the topic. Look at the sentence below, paying close attention to the underlined words:

> They were readily **manipulated** by **unscrupulous** employers, politicians, criminals, and landlords.

In this sentence, the words *manipulated* (i.e., managed and controlled in an unfair way) and *unscrupulous* (i.e., unprincipled) both have an extremely negative impact upon the reader. The use of these two words reveals the writer's sympathetic attitude toward immigrants.

TASK 21: Look at the following words, taken from "The Huddled Masses." Scan the reading and locate the sentence in which each of these words appears. Use a dictionary to determine the meaning, or denotation, of each word. Then, based on the context of the sentence, decide if the word has a positive or a negative connotation. Mark your choice in the appropriate column. The first one has been done for you.

Word	Meaning	Positive	Negative
1. array (¶ 7)	an impressively large number	X	
2. bedraggled (¶ 4)			
3. distorted (¶ 4)			
4. expel (¶ 4)			
5. herded (¶ 6)			
6. impersonal (¶ 6)			
7. lenient (¶ 3)			
8. poetic (¶ 4)			
9. stir (¶ 4)			
10. turmoil (¶ 3)			
11. wise (¶ 7)			

TASK 22: Read the sentences below. Rewrite each one, using synonyms for the words in boldface. Maintain the connotation of the original sentence.

1. Original sentence: The majority of the people in southern and eastern Europe—people who did *not* leave for America—are **evidence** that such an **array** of **choices** existed.

   <u>Southern and Eastern Europeans—those who chose not to emigrate—are proof</u>
   <u>that there was a range of possibilities other than immigration to America.</u>

2. Original sentence: They are pitied as **bedraggled** wayfarers, expelled from their homelands by **vast** social forces beyond their comprehension or control, **driven to** emigrate and attracted to America by the **blandishments** of profit-seeking land agents and entrepreneurs.

   _____

   _____

   _____

3. Original sentence: The general reader, informed by journalists, television producers, and politicians, **clings** to a **simplistic** and **distorted** image of the **newcomers**.

   _____

   _____

   _____

Integrating Perspectives

APPLYING THE CONCEPTS

Three of the sources in this chapter—the lecture by Professor Laslett, the poem by Emma Lazarus, and "The Huddled Masses" by Alan M. Kraut—present differing views of the immigrant. We can label these views "the romanticized hero/heroine," "the uprooted victim," and "the independent individual."

TASK 23: Use the three sources to find details that explain these three views. Fill in the charts with the relevant details and identify the source for each detail. An example has been provided for you.

UPROOTED VICTIM	
DETAIL	**SOURCE**
victims of powerful historical forces such as war and famine	Laslett

ROMANTICIZED HERO/HEROINE	
DETAIL	**SOURCE**

INDEPENDENT INDIVIDUAL	
DETAIL	**SOURCE**

ANALYZING THROUGH DISCUSSION

Consider the views about immigrants in the chart above and think of an immigrant group that you are familiar with.

TASK 24: Decide which of the three views best fits the immigrant group you have chosen. Why? Share this information in small groups.

EVALUATING THROUGH WRITING

At the beginning of this unit, immigration was defined as the movement of people over distance, often across political boundaries. Although not all people have experienced immigration, most people have experienced changes in their lives, such as moving from a village to a city or changing cities, schools, or professions. All of these moves require adjustments and may result in personal changes that are similar to those experienced by immigrants on a larger scale.

TASK 25: Write a short essay about an experience you have had that involved a significant change. Why did you make this change? What effects did this change have on your life? How have you changed as a result?

EXPLORATION:
TRADITIONAL MODELS
OF ASSIMILATION

This chapter examines two traditional models of assimilation theory, *total assimilation* and *amalgamation,* through academic readings and lectures from an American history course.

Exploring the Concepts

EXPLORING THROUGH WRITING

The discussion of immigration in the last chapter was based on your background knowledge and a variety of sources. This chapter focuses on how immigrants become part of, or assimilate into, a new culture.

TASK 1: Write a journal entry describing some of the challenges immigrants encounter. Base this response on your own experiences or the experiences of someone you know.

Targeting Vocabulary: Word Families

TASK 2: The following are words from the readings in this unit. Using a dictionary, look up the meaning of each word in the column on the left. Provide the missing members of each word family. The first one has been done for you.

	VERB	NOUN	ADJECTIVE/PARTICIPLE
assimilate	to assimilate	assimilation	assimilated
achieve			
amalgamate			
blend			
decline			
decrease			
encourage			
increase			
perceive			
require			
retain			

EXPLORING THROUGH DISCUSSION

A *poll* is the result of questioning or surveying the opinions of a sample group of people. The people are carefully selected to represent a number of different opinions. Look carefully at and analyze the following poll about immigration and the melting pot. This poll was taken by *Newsweek* magazine.

Newsweek Poll

Was immigration a good thing or a bad thing for this country in the past?
    59%   Good thing
    31%   Bad thing

Is immigration a good thing or a bad thing for this country today?
    29%   Good thing
    60%   Bad thing

Is the United States still a melting pot, or do immigrants today maintain their national identity more strongly?
    20%   Still a melting pot
    66%   Maintain identity

Source: (1983, August 9). *Newsweek,* (p. 19).

TASK 3: Using the information from the poll, discuss the following questions with a partner:

1. Have American attitudes toward immigration changed?

2. What is meant by a melting pot?

3. Do the majority of those interviewed view the United States as a melting pot?

Working with Sources

UNDERSTANDING THROUGH READING 1

The following brief reading from a sociology textbook defines assimilation. Some of the terms in this excerpt will be expanded in the sources that follow.

TASK 4: As you read "Assimilation," focus on the differences between behavioral assimilation and structural assimilation.

ASSIMILATION

Alex Thio

[1]   Frequently, a minority group accepts the culture of the dominant group, fading into the larger society. This process, called *assimilation,* has at least two aspects. The first is *behavioral assimilation,* which means that the minority group adopts the dominant culture—its language, values, norms, and so on—giving up its own distinctive characteristics. Behavioral assimilation, however, does not guarantee *structural assimilation*—in which the minority group ceases to be a minority *and* is accepted on equal terms with the rest of society. German-Americans, for example, have achieved structural assimilation, but African-Americans have not. Taken as a whole, assimilation can be expressed as A + B + C = A, where minorities (B and C) lose their subcultural traits and become indistinguishable from the dominant group (A) (Newman, 1973).

[2]   When the dominant group is ethnocentric, believing that its subculture is superior to others', then minority groups face considerable pressure to achieve behavioral assimilation. How easily they make this transition depends on both their attitude toward their own subculture and the degree of similarity between themselves and the dominant group. Minority groups that take pride in their own subculture are likely to resist behavioral assimilation. This may explain why Jews and Asians in the United States display "an unusual degree of ethnic solidarity" (Hirschman, 1983). Groups that are very different from the dominant group may find that even behavioral assimilation does not lead to structural assimilation.

Source: (1991). *Sociology: A brief introduction* (pp. 421–422). New York: HarperCollins.

TASK 5: Below are examples of immigrant groups living in a variety of host countries. Next to each description of the immigrant group and its assimilation pattern, write NA (nonassimilated), BA (behavioral assimilation), or SA (structural assimilation) to indicate which type of assimilation pattern this group exhibits. The first one is done for you as an example.

_SA_ 1. The Scandinavian immigrants who became farmers in Minnesota blend in with all the other northern European immigrants living in that area.

_____ 2. Chinese immigrants living in Indonesia go to separate Chinese schools; they cannot hold political office. Intermarriage with the Indonesian host culture is discouraged.

_____ 3. Third-generation Mexican–Americans living in Los Angeles generally think of themselves as Californians rather than Mexican; they seldom speak Spanish, practice very few Mexican customs, and most of their friends are Anglo. They are active in civic and political organizations.

_____ 4. Turkish migrant workers living in Germany do not speak German fluently; they live together in their own ethnic neighborhoods, and the women maintain their traditional dress.

_____ 5. East Indians living in Kenya and other parts of East Africa speak Swahili, the dominant language of the area; they interact extensively with other members of the local community but ethnically they remain distinct.

_____ 6. Japanese immigrants in Peru live and work together with members of the host culture; they speak only Spanish, and many have assumed positions of political power (including high governmental offices).

TASK 6: In groups, brainstorm one other example of an immigrant group and decide which type of assimilation pattern this group displays. Share this information with the rest of the class.

UNDERSTANDING THROUGH READING 2

In this article, "Assimilation in American Life," Milton Gordon creates two hypothetical groups, Sylvanians and Mundovians. He discusses how the Mundovians immigrated and assimilated into Sylvanian society.

TASK 7: Before you read, preview the text, paying attention to the chart on the next page that summarizes Gordon's idealized seven stages of assimilation.

TASK 8: As you read the text, pay special attention to what the Mundovians must give up and what the Sylvanians must do to accommodate the Mundovians.

ASSIMILATION IN AMERICAN LIFE

Milton Gordon

[1]   Let us, first of all, imagine a hypothetical situation in which a host country, to which we shall give the fictitious name of "Sylvania," is made up of a population all members of which are of the same race, religion, and previous national extraction. Cultural behavior is relatively uniform except for social class divisions. Similarly, the groups and institutions, i.e., the "social structure," of Sylvanian society are divided and differentiated only on a social class basis. Into this country, through immigration, comes a group of people who differ in previous national background and in religion and who thus have different cultural patterns from those of the host society. We shall call them the Mundovians. Let us further imagine that within the span of another generation, this population group of Mundovian national origin (now composed largely of the second generation, born in Sylvania) has taken on completely the cultural patterns of the Sylvanians, has thrown off any sense of peoplehood based on Mundovian nationality, has changed its religion to that of the Sylvanians, has eschewed the formation of any communal organizations made up principally or exclusively of Mundovians, has entered and been hospitably accepted into the social cliques, clubs, and institutions of the Sylvanians at various class levels, has intermarried freely and frequently with the Sylvanians, encounters no prejudice or discrimination (one reason being that they are no longer distinguishable culturally or structurally from the rest of the Sylvanian population), and raises no value conflict issues in Sylvanian public life. Such a situation would represent the ultimate form of assimilation—complete assimilation to the culture and society of the host country. Note that we are making no judgment here of either the sociological desirability, feasibility, or moral rightness of such a goal. We are simply setting it up as a convenient abstraction—an "ideal type"—ideal not in the value sense of being most desirable but in the sense of representing the various elements of the concept and their interrelationships in "pure," or unqualified, fashion (the methodological device of the "ideal type" was developed and named by the German sociologist Max Weber).

[2]   Looking at this example, we may discern that seven major variables are involved in the process discussed—in other words, seven basic subprocesses have taken place in the assimilation of the Mundovians to Sylvanian society. These may be listed in the following manner. We may say that the Mundovians have

1) changed their cultural patterns (including religious belief and observance) to those of the Sylvanians;

2) taken on large-scale primary group relationships with the Sylvanians, i.e., have entered fully into the societal network of groups and institutions, or societal structure, of the Sylvanians;

3) have intermarried and interbred fully with the Sylvanians;

4) have developed a Sylvanian, in place of a Mundovian, sense of peoplehood, or ethnicity;

5) do not raise by their demands concerning the nature of Sylvanian public or civic life, any issues involving value and power conflict with the original Sylvanians (for example, the issue of birth control);

6) have reached a point where they encounter no prejudiced attitudes;

7) have reached a point where they encounter no discriminatory behavior.

[3]   Each of these steps or subprocesses may be thought of as constituting a particular stage or aspect of the assimilation process. Thus we may, in shorthand fashion, consider them as types of assimilation and characterize them accordingly. We may, then, speak, for

TYPE OR STAGE OF ASSIMILATION	SUBPROCESS OR CONDITION	SPECIAL TERM
1. Cultural or behavioral assimilation	Change of cultural patterns to those of host society	Acculturation
2. Structural assimilation	Large-scale entrance into cliques, clubs, and institutions of host society, on primary group level	None
3. Marital assimilation	Large-scale intermarriage	Amalgamation
4. Identificational assimilation	Development of sense of peoplehood based exclusively on host society	None
5. Civic assimilation	Absence of value and power conflict	None
6. Attitude receptional assimilation	Absence of prejudice	None
7. Behavior receptional assimilation	Absence of discrimination	None

instance, of "structural assimilation" to refer to the entrance of Mundovians into primary group relationships with the Sylvanians, or "identificational assimilation" to describe the taking on of a sense of Sylvanian peoplehood. For some of the particular assimilation subprocesses there are existing special terms, already reviewed. For instance, cultural or behavioral assimilation is what has already been defined as "acculturation." The full list of assimilation subprocesses or variables with their general names, and special names, if any, is given in the table [above].

[4]   Not only is the assimilation process mainly a matter of degree, but, obviously, each of the stages or subprocesses distinguished above may take place in varying degrees.

Source: (1964). *Assimilation in American life* (pp. 68–71). New York: Oxford University Press.

TASK 9: The example of the Sylvanians and the Mundovians is a *hypothetical* example, invented to illustrate what happens in the real world. Many countries have a dominant ethnic or religious group and a population of immigrants from one or more other countries. Think of an immigrant group you are familiar with—your own or another. In small groups, present your answers to the following questions. Be sure to take notes on your classmates' answers.

1. What group are you discussing?

2. What has this group given up in order to assimilate? Give examples.

3. How has the group's status changed over the years?

4. Is this group's assimilation into the dominant culture similar to or different from the Mundovians' assimilation? Give examples.

UNDERSTANDING THROUGH LISTENING 1

Lecture: Models of Assimilation
Segment 2: Variables of Assimilation

Professor: John Laslett
Course: History 160: The Immigrant in America
Text: *Assimilation in American Life* by Milton Gordon

As he begins his lecture, Professor Laslett refers to the seven stages of assimilation that Gordon presents in his book.

TASK 10: Fill in the diagram as you watch the lecture by Professor Laslett. An example has been done for you. Watch as many times as necessary to complete the task.

"MUNDOVIANS" OR IMMIGRANT GROUP

1. Cultural assimilation

Irish give up soccer and play American football.

2. Structural assimilation

3. Marital assimilation

4. Identificational assimilation

"SYLVANIANS" OR HOST GROUP

5. Civic assimilation

6. Attitude receptional assimilation

7. Behavior receptional assimilation

TASK 11: Read the cases below and decide which of Gordon's seven stages of assimilation apply. Provide explanations on separate paper. Note that more than one stage of assimilation may apply to each case. An example has been done for you.

GORDON'S SEVEN STAGES OF ASSIMILATION

1. Cultural assimilation
2. Structural assimilation
3. Intermarriage
4. Attitude/identity = peoplehood
5. Civic assimilation = values are shared with the host society
6. Encounter no prejudiced attitudes
7. Encounter no discriminatory behavior

1. Jewish immigrants to the United States come from all over the world. Some strictly observe Jewish religious practices and customs after they come to the United States, even though many American Jews tend to be less religiously observant.

   Explanation: This is an example of a lack of cultural assimilation because these Jewish people have not assimilated into American culture. Some Jewish people who immigrate to the U.S. value their religion more than cultural and structural assimilation. They keep their religious beliefs and practices even though other American Jews in the mainstream may not strictly maintain traditional religious practices.

2. In recent years, more and more people with Hispanic surnames have been elected to the Congress of the United States and appointed to other positions. For example, Henry Cisneros, a Latino American, was appointed by President Clinton to serve as Secretary of Housing and Urban Development.

3. Many children of first-generation immigrants do not speak their parents' native language. Instead, they speak the language used in the host country's schools and public institutions.

4. Before the outbreak of World War II, Chinese and Japanese immigrants were not allowed to become citizens of the United States even if they had lived in the United States for over twenty years and raised children here who were citizens. On the other hand, immigrants from Germany were allowed to apply for citizenship immediately.

5. When asked what nationality they are, most new immigrants from Korea state that they are Koreans. Those who are second-generation immigrants, however, often state that they are Americans.

6. A family lives on the Navajo reservation in New Mexico. The wife is 100 percent Navajo while the husband is Anglo. One of their sons married an Anglo, lives in Washington, and works for the Bureau of Indian Affairs. The other son, a physician, is married to a Navajo woman. They live on the same reservation as her parents.

7. In several cultures of the world, it is the custom that women's bodies must be covered. These women must wear long skirts and blouses with long sleeves and high collars. When these same women raise their children in the United States, their daughters often do not continue to practice this custom, instead preferring to dress like other young American women.

Targeting Grammar: Brief Definitions through Relative Clauses

Often in academic writing, authors use specific phrases and structures to introduce brief definitions of terms. One strategy is the use of *relative clauses*, which are created by combining two simple sentences into one complex sentence joined by a relative pronoun. To construct a brief definition with a relative clause, locate the term or idea that the two sentences have in common. Follow these steps to determine which relative pronoun to use:

- If the repeated term is the subject in the second sentence, use the subject pronouns *who, which,* or *that.*

- If the repeated term is the object of a verb in the second sentence, use the object pronouns *whom, which,* or *that.*

Because the relative clause contains additional, not essential, information, it is set off by commas. By combining simple sentences with relative clauses, good writers are able to use complex sentences to avoid unnecessary repetition. Study the following chart. Note how the definition combines the information from sentences one and two.

SENTENCE ONE	+	SENTENCE TWO	=	DEFINITION
The first variable is *behavioral assimilation.*	+	*Behavioral assimilation* means the minority group adopts the majority culture.	=	The first variable is behavioral assimilation, **which** means the minority group adopts the majority culture.
Members of the second generation often have a limited command of their parents' native language.	+	*Members of the second generation* are the children of immigrants.	=	Members of the second generation, **who** are the children of immigrants, often have a limited command of their parents' native language.
Henry Cisneros is Latino-American.	+	President Clinton appointed *Henry Cisneros* to serve as Secretary of Housing and Urban Development.	=	Henry Cisneros, **whom** President Clinton appointed to serve as Secretary of Housing and Urban Development, is Latino-American.

TASK 12: Look at the examples below and determine the two sentences that have been combined to create the definition:

SENTENCE ONE	+	SENTENCE TWO	=	DEFINITION
1.	+		=	Emma Lazarus, **who** wrote the poem at the foot of the Statue of Liberty, intended her poem to be an invitation to immigrants.
2.	+		=	Behavioral assimilation does not guarantee structural assimilation, **in which** the minority group ceases to be a minority and is accepted on equal terms with the rest of society.
3.	+		=	Amalgamation produces a "melting pot," **in which** many subcultures are blended together to produce a new culture, one that differs from any of its components.
4.	+		=	Cultural assimilation, **which** does not happen in one generation, means that the immigrant group gives up its native language, religion, diet, and dress.
5.	+		=	The United States has been called a nation of immigrants, **which** means that everyone here came from somewhere else.
6.	+		=	The Mundovians, **who** gave up everything to integrate into the Sylvanian culture, are an example of total assimilation.

Task 13: Using the information you have learned from the readings and the videotaped lecture, write brief definitions for Gordon's seven variables for assimilation. The first one is done for you.

1. cultural assimilation: <u>Cultural assimilation, which does not happen in one generation,</u>

<u>means that the immigrant group gives up its native language, religion, diet, and dress.</u>

2. structural assimilation: _____

_____

_____

3. marital assimilation: _____

_____

_____

4. identificational assimilation: _____

_____

_____

5. civic assimilation: _____

_____

_____

6. attitude receptional assimilation: _____

_____

_____

7. behavior receptional assimilation: _____

_____

_____

VIDEO

UNDERSTANDING THROUGH LISTENING 2

Lecture: Models of Assimilation
Segment 3: The Melting Pot Model

Professor: John Laslett
Course: History 160: The Immigrant in America
Text: *Assimilation in American Life* by Milton Gordon

In this lecture, Professor Laslett describes a second model of assimilation theory: the *melting pot*, or *amalgamation* model. According to this model, both the host society and the incoming immigrant group give up certain cultural elements, which correspond to Gordon's seven variables of assimilation. Professor Laslett uses a graphic organizer to explain how this theory works.

TASK 14: Study the diagram below before watching Professor Laslett's lecture. What do you imagine this lecture will be about?

GORDON'S SEVEN VARIABLES FOR ASSIMILATION

1. Cultural assimilation
2. Structural assimilation
3. Intermarriage
4. Attitude/identity = peoplehood
5. Civic assimilation = values are shared with the host society
6. Encounter no discriminatory behavior
7. Encounter no prejudiced attitudes

Incoming Mundovians
(give up four variables)

Host Sylvanians
(give up three variables)

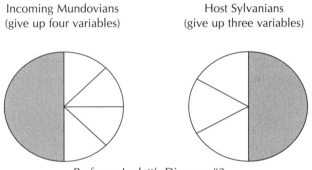

Professor Laslett's Diagram #2

TASK 15: Watch the lecture by Professor Laslett. He says that the second-generation Americans had characteristics that were different from the European groups from which their parents had come. What are the characteristics of the new group created by the mixing of the two populations? Check the characteristics that Professor Laslett mentions.

- ☐ sensitive
- ☐ happy
- ☐ outgoing
- ☐ deferential
- ☐ obedient

- ☐ angry
- ☐ fatalistic
- ☐ realistic
- ☐ idealistic
- ☐ assertive

- ☐ uppity
- ☐ progressive
- ☐ pensive
- ☐ optimistic
- ☐ conscious

TASK 16: Watch the lecture again. On separate paper take notes on the main ideas about the melting pot theory.

TASK 17: Professor Laslett does not specifically state the characteristics of the original European groups. What do you imagine these characteristics were? Discuss them with your group. To help you, refer to the previous lectures and readings in this unit.

Targeting Vocabulary: Synonyms

Each of the characteristics of the "new American" that you identified in Task 15 takes the form of an adjective. Each adjective has many synonyms.

TASK 18: Look at the headings in the chart below. Find the adjectives that have the same or similar meanings in the list under the chart. Write these adjectives in the chart under the appropriate heading. Use a dictionary if necessary. Discuss your choices with a classmate. The first one is done for you.

OPTIMISTIC	ASSERTIVE	UPPITY
rosy		

FATALISTIC	CONSCIOUS	DEFERENTIAL

bossy	promising	pessimistic	obedient
passive	morose	aware	negative
authoritative	subservient	stuck-up	sensitive
~~rosy~~	commanding	conceited	arrogant
cheerful	positive	despairing	vain
perceptive	sanguine	accepting	cognizant

UNDERSTANDING THROUGH READING 3

The United States is often called a melting pot. Because it is one of the largest nations of immigrants in the world, in the United States the model of amalgamation may characterize the way in which immigrants are accepted into the society.

TASK 19: As you read the following article, highlight the main ideas.

AMALGAMATION

Alex Thio

[1]   A society which believes that groups should go through the process of behavioral assimilation in order to be accepted as equals obviously has little respect for the distinctive traits of these groups. In contrast, a society that seeks amalgamation as an ideal has some appreciation for the equal worth of various subcultures. *Amalgamation* produces a "melting pot," in which many subcultures are blended together to produce a

new culture, one that differs from any of its components. Like assimilation, amalgamation requires groups to give up their distinct racial and ethnic identities. But unlike assimilation, amalgamation demands respect for the original subcultures. Various groups are expected to contribute their own subcultures to the development of a new culture, without pushing any one subculture at the expense of another. Usually, this blending of diverse subcultures results from intermarriage. It can be described as A + B + C = D, where A, B, and C represent different groups jointly producing a new culture (D) unlike any of its original components (Newman, 1973).

[2]   More than 70 years ago a British-Jewish dramatist portrayed the United States as an amalgamation of subcultures. "There she lies," he wrote, "the great melting pot—listen! . . . Ah, what a stirring and seething—Celt and Latin, Slav and Teuton, Greek and Syrian, Black and Yellow—Jew and Gentile" (Zangwill 1909). Indeed, to some extent America is a melting pot. In popular music and slang, for example, you can find elements of many subcultures.

Source: (1991). *Sociology: A brief introduction* (pp. 421–422). New York: HarperCollins.

SUMMARIES IN ACADEMIC WRITING

Summaries are often found in academic work. As a student, you will be asked to read and listen to summaries; you will also have to write summaries on essay exams and in term papers.

SUMMARIES AS STUDY TOOLS

A summary can be a helpful study tool, a learning or memory aid for information presented in readings or lectures. Summarizing accomplishes several things:

- It provides an accurate and concise understanding of the main ideas.
- It shows you how the ideas you summarized fit with the other ideas you have already learned.
- It allows you to write and think critically about these ideas.

THE PROCESS OF SUMMARIZING

To write a good summary, you must be able to determine which ideas are important and which are not. You must also be able to see how all the important ideas relate to each other. To write a summary:

- Read the text more than once and take notes.
- Without looking at the text, restate the main ideas in *your own words*.
- Look at the text again to check that you have included the most important points. Be sure that you haven't changed the author's ideas.

ACADEMIC STRATEGY:

SUMMARIZING

TASK 20: In the paragraph below, certain parts of the text have been crossed out as a preliminary step to summarizing. Examine the text to see which pieces of information have been crossed out. Discuss why the remaining information would be important in a summary.

~~A society which believes that groups should go through the process of behavioral assimilation in order to be accepted as equals obviously has little respect for the distinctive traits of these groups. In contrast,~~ a society that seeks amalgamation ~~as an ideal~~ has some appreciation for the equal worth of various subcultures. **Amalgamation** produces a "melting pot," in which many subcultures are blended together to produce a new culture, one that differs from any of its components. ~~Like~~

~~assimilation~~, amalgamation requires groups to give up their distinct racial and ethnic identities. ~~But unlike assimilation,~~ amalgamation demands respect for the original subcultures. ~~Various~~ groups ~~are expected to~~ contribute ~~their own subcultures~~ to the development of a new culture, without pushing any one subculture at the expense of another. ~~Usually,~~ this blending of diverse subcultures results from intermarriage. ~~It can be described as A + B + C = D, where A, B, and C represent different groups jointly producing a new culture (D) unlike any of its original components (Newman, 1973).~~

TASK 21: Read the following paragraph. Cross out the sentences and ideas that you would not include in a summary.

More than 70 years ago a British-Jewish dramatist portrayed the United States as an amalgamation of subcultures. "There she lies," he wrote, "the great melting pot— listen! . . . Ah, what a stirring and seething—Celt and Latin, Slav and Teuton, Greek and Syrian, Black and Yellow—Jew and Gentile" (Zangwill 1909). Indeed, to some extent America is a melting pot. In popular music and slang, for example, you can find elements of many subcultures.

TASK 22: Using the information that remains in the article on amalgamation in Tasks 20 and 21, write a one-paragraph summary of amalgamation. Then compare your summary with those of your classmates.

Integrating Perspectives

APPLYING THE CONCEPTS 1

TASK 23: Immigrants give up many aspects of home life and culture as they attempt to assimilate into a new culture and society. Rank the following six aspects of life and culture that immigrants give up. In your opinion, which would be the easiest to give up? Rank it as number 1. Which would be the second easiest? Rank it as number 2, and so on until you have numbered each aspect. Be prepared to give reasons for your choices.

_____ a. Cultural patterns (practices and habits) that are determined by "home" culture

_____ b. Language

_____ c. Primary group relationships with people from own culture and country

_____ d. Marrying and having children with a person from own cultural group

_____ e. Identity or personhood based on "home" culture

_____ f. Values and ideals determined by "home" culture

TASK 24: Compare your rankings with those of your classmates. Which items did you rank similarly? Which did you rank differently? Why?

ANALYZING THROUGH VISUAL IMAGES

TASK 25: Complete one of the following activities on a separate piece of paper.

1. Draw a visual representation of the melting pot and explain it to your classmates.

2. Diagram the two different models of assimilation: total assimilation and amalgamation. Explain the differences between the diagrams to your classmates.

APPLYING THE CONCEPTS 2

TASK 26: Complete the following chart to compare and contrast the two models of immigration you have learned about: total assimilation and amalgamation. The first question has been answered for you.

	TOTAL ASSIMILATION	AMALGAMATION (MELTING POT)
1. What do new immigrants give up?	• their religion • their language • their identity or peoplehood • customs from their homeland • membership in groups from their homeland	• some of their religious practices • their language in some contexts (i.e., they may speak their language at home but not in public places) • some of their identity or peoplehood • some customs from their homeland • membership in some groups from their homeland
2. How does the host culture react to new immigrants?		
3. When is a new immigrant fully accepted in this model?		
4. What factors contribute to acceptance?		
5. What are the problems with this model?		

EVALUATING THROUGH WRITING

TASK 27: Write a brief summary in which you compare total assimilation and amalgamation. Use the information in the chart you completed in Task 26.

EXPANSION:
RECOGNIZING DIVERSITY

Two recent models of assimilation theory presented in this chapter are cultural pluralism and the triple-generation theory. A short story written by the daughter of Chinese immigrants who settled in California will illustrate these two models.

Exploring the Concepts

EXPLORING THROUGH VISUAL IMAGES

In the Introduction and Exploration chapters of this unit, you explored some of the historical views of immigration, including looking at the poem by Emma Lazarus that is inscribed on the base of the Statue of Liberty. This cartoon offers a contrast to her poem:

TASK 1: How does the cartoon contrast with Lazarus's poem? What does this cartoon suggest about the ways that U.S. citizens' attitudes about immigration and immigrants have changed? Discuss these questions in small groups.

TASK 2: The cartoon drawing at left of the Statue of Liberty has no quotation. Write a quotation or caption that reflects what you think today's attitudes are towards immigration, immigration policy, or the idea of the melting pot. Justify what you write based on the articles you have read, the lectures you have viewed, and your class discussions.

EXPLORING BACKGROUND KNOWLEDGE

Through the academic source readings and the lectures by Professor Laslett in this unit, you have learned about two models of assimilation: total assimilation and amalgamation (the melting pot). The diagrams below summarize these two models.

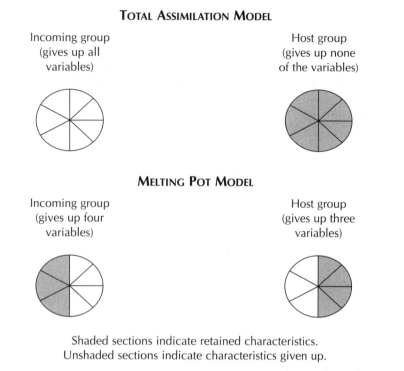

TOTAL ASSIMILATION MODEL

Incoming group
(gives up all
variables)

Host group
(gives up none
of the variables)

MELTING POT MODEL

Incoming group
(gives up four
variables)

Host group
(gives up three
variables)

Shaded sections indicate retained characteristics.
Unshaded sections indicate characteristics given up.

Source: Professor John Laslett's lecture notes

TASK 3: Think of a person you know whose assimilation experience does not fit one of these models. Describe the situation to a partner or a small group.

TASK 4: In small groups, construct a third model that represents another type of assimilation experience and fits the person you described in Task 3. Share your group's model with the rest of the class.

Working with Sources

UNDERSTANDING THROUGH READING

Many historians feel that the models of assimilation studied thus far are too limited and do not reflect the reality of today's ethnic diversity of the United States. Recently, another model, *cultural pluralism*, has been proposed.

TASK 5: In the reading that follows, the author uses the examples of Switzerland and the United States to contrast cultural pluralism with assimilation and amalgamation. Alex Thio uses the strategy of negative definition, that is, defining what cultural pluralism is *not* rather than what it *is*. As you read the passage, focus on the elements of Alex Thio's negative definition.

CULTURAL PLURALISM

Alex Thio

[1]   Switzerland provides an example of yet a third way in which ethnic groups may live together. In Switzerland, three major groups—Germans, French, and Italians—retain their own languages while living together in peace. They are neither assimilated nor amalgamated. Instead, these diverse groups retain their distinctive subcultures while coexisting peacefully. This situation is called cultural pluralism. It is the opposite of assimilation and requires yet greater mutual respect for other groups' traditions and customs than does amalgamation. And unlike either assimilation or amalgamation, cultural pluralism encourages each group to take pride in its distinctiveness, to be conscious of its heritage, and to retain its identity. Such pluralism can be shown as A + B + C = A + B + C, where various groups continue to keep their subcultures while living together in the same society (Newman, 1973).

[2]   To some extent, the United States has long been marked by cultural pluralism. This can be seen in the Chinatowns, Little Italies, and Polish neighborhoods of many American cities. These ethnic enclaves owe their existence more to discrimination than to the respectful encouragement of diversity that characterizes true pluralism.

[3]   For many groups in America, cultural pluralism has become a goal. This became evident during the 1960s and 1970s, when blacks and white ethnics alike denounced assimilation and proclaimed pride in their own identities. But pluralism is not easy to maintain. It requires that society conquer prejudice and respect various groups equally. If it fails to do so, pluralism is likely to give way to either assimilation or outright rejection of minority groups.

Source: (1991). *Sociology: A brief introduction* (pp. 421–422). New York: HarperCollins.

TASK 6: Answer the following questions to check your comprehension of the passage:

1. According to Thio, what are the three positive characteristics of cultural pluralism as exemplified by Switzerland?

2. What negative factor has created cultural pluralism in the United States?

3. Why is cultural pluralism difficult to maintain?

TASK 7: In his lectures, Professor Laslett referred to graphic models of the theories he presented. On a separate piece of paper, create a graphic representation to capture the idea of cultural pluralism and explain it to your classmates.

TASK 8: Think of an ethnic group—your own or another. Write a journal entry in which you respond to the following questions:

1. How does the model of cultural pluralism fit the group you have chosen?

2. What are the strengths of this model?

3. What are the weaknesses of this model?

4. As an accurate representation of how this group fits into the host society, how does the model of cultural pluralism compare with the models of total assimilation and amalgamation?

UNDERSTANDING THROUGH LISTENING

VIDEO

> **Lecture:** Models of Assimilation
> **Segment 4:** Triple Generation Theory
>
> **Professor:** John Laslett
> **Course:** History 160: The Immigrant in America

In this next part of Professor Laslett's lecture, he goes beyond the three models of assimilation—total assimilation, melting pot/amalgamation, and cultural pluralism—to present another model, the *triple generation theory*. According to this theory, assimilation is a process that happens over time and over successive generations.

TASK 9: As you watch the lecture, take notes on the main ideas on a separate piece of paper. Note that as Professor Laslett begins, the two theories he is referring to are the total assimilation theory and the melting pot theory.

TASK 10: Use your lecture notes to complete the chart and answer the questions that follow it. Watch the lecture as many times as necessary to complete the task.

TRIPLE GENERATION THEORY

FIRST GENERATION ↓	SECOND GENERATION ↓	THIRD GENERATION ↓
identifies with:	identifies with:	identifies with:

1. Does total assimilation happen? If so, to whom?

_____

_____

2. What variables determine the degree of assimilation?

_____

_____

3. Professor Laslett does not expand on these variables. How do you think they work in determining the degree of assimilation? Illustrate your response with examples from your own experiences or those of someone you know.

_____

_____

Integrating Perspectives

ANALYZING THROUGH DISCUSSION

ACADEMIC STRATEGY: APPLYING A THEORY TO A CASE	In order to see how accurately a theory may apply, researchers often conduct *case studies*. In a case study, an individual or group of individuals is interviewed about experiences related to the theory. These interviews are often personal and follow a set of open-ended questions, so that the individual can freely describe his or her situation.

TASK 11: To examine the triple generation theory, create a set of questions to ask individuals from different ethnic backgrounds about their family histories.

- First, think of four or five open-ended questions. For ideas about what questions to ask, you may want to review the readings and lectures in this unit. Focus your questions on the assimilation experience of different generations in the individual's family.
- Write the questions in the spaces provided below. One example has been done for you.

1. <u>Where were you born?</u> _____

2. _____

3. _____

4. _____

5. _____

TASK 12: Interview two people outside of class. If possible, try to find people who are of different ethnic backgrounds from your own. Take careful notes during the interviews and use the information to write a brief summary of each person's assimilation history.

Example:

Ingrid Jensen was born in Los Angeles in 1952. Her parents moved there from Wisconsin before Ingrid was born. Although Ingrid's parents were both born in the United States, their parents (Ingrid's grandparents) were from Denmark. Ingrid's grandparents spoke only Danish at home; however, Ingrid's father speaks English and can understand only limited Danish. Ingrid's mother can still speak Danish, but speaks to her children only in English. Despite their Danish heritage, Ingrid's parents have never been to Denmark; Ingrid has traveled to Denmark to meet some of her relatives, and is currently studying Danish in the evenings. Ingrid's family is an example of the triple-generation theory.

TASK 13: In small groups or with a partner, compare the findings of your case studies. Here are a few suggested questions. Add others of your own.

1. In which generations do family members speak only the language of the country of origin? In which generations do they speak only English? In which generations do they speak both?
2. Has intercultural marriage occurred in this family? Has it been successful?
3. Is this family an example of the triple generation theory? Why or why not?

EVALUATING THROUGH LITERATURE

Genny Lim is the daughter of Chinese immigrants in California. She writes about the conflicts in culture and identity faced by children of immigrants, or second-generation immigrants. The text begins with a dream that she had about finding Chinese artifacts in a museum and singing Chinese opera.

TASK 14: As you read Genny Lim's story, think about how the four assimilation models apply to Genny and her parents.

A JUK-SING OPERA

Genny Lim

[1]   I had this dream where I was inside a museum surrounded by ancient Chinese artifacts. The feeling of reverence and exaltation was great each time I discovered a precious object retrieved from memory or association. Silk garments with hand-embroidered dragons and phoenixes, porcelain cups, opium pipes, a hand-carved camphor chest with intricate motifs, jade and ivory carvings, vases once touched, possessed or seen in the past and long forgotten. Discovering an old rattan trunk, the type my uncle might have brought to Angel Island, I am moved to ecstasy and suddenly break into song.

[2]   The music that emerges from my mouth, however, fills me with amazement. I am singing Cantonese opera! It's as if I'm possessed by another being. My voice rises and falls in a familiar falsetto. The only time I have heard such virtuosos singing like this was as a little girl at the Great Star Theater, where the traveling operas came once a year. They, too, had to stay on Angel Island each time they came to tour. In fact, they entertained the detainees to alleviate their depression and boredom. The crowds in *Die-Fow* (San Francisco) loved them so much they would shower them with fabulous collars made of dollar bills. Now I become their idol, singing like a Hung-Sung-Nui, the famous opera star, with every soul rapt in my hand's palm. My phrasing and timing are precise, my tone clear and shrill like a flute as my voice slides through a series of varying pitches on the same syllable, turning vocal cartwheels in steep-falling rhythmic cadences.

[3]   I awaken and the opera vanishes. The illusion of transcendence and self-mastery is suddenly gone. I'm still a tongue-tied *hu-ji nuey*, an American-born Chinese girl in San Francisco.

[4]   But I can still hear the opera echoing in my ears. Its lyrical melody lingers, leading me like the zigzagging line on a highway may to a destination unknown.

[5]   As the youngest of seven children, I often felt removed from any sense of a cultural past. As a second generation American-born Chinese, I was often a living contradiction of dual values and identities. At home, my Chinese-ness gave way, much to mother's sadness, to American-ness; and outside, my American-ness always belied my Chinese sensibility. If the twain theoretically never met, they certainly often collided for me.

[6]   As a little girl, I bristled with shame and outrage as I heard people call my father "Chinaman." Yet his erect, proud bearing never betrayed any anger or humiliation. And I now realize the alienation that pride cost him. Because of his need for the secure kinship of fellow villagers, father never left Chinatown. He would not hear mother's constant cry to leave the ghetto for the suburbs of the city. One of the very few places where he did take us was the Sacramento Delta.

[7]   In the old days it would take Pop about four hours to wind his way through the highways to the delta. Perhaps the trip took so long because of his growing confusion over the new freeways that kept springing up overnight. Our out-of-town trips trickled to about one a year for only special clan occasions, like the Bomb Day celebration in Marysville, where a frenzy of over-zealous young men vied for the coveted prizes that signified the

appeasement of the goddess, *Bok Kai*, thrown into a crowded square. Sometimes fights would erupt over the cylindrical, red-wrapped prizes, which contained a gold ring, and sometimes we would get jostled or stepped on. Once in the melee I cried in terror as I was knocked to the ground. Maybe *Bok Kai* could ward off floods, but she didn't seem effective against stampedes.

[8]   Father was part-owner of the Golden Lantern Restaurant in Sacramento. All I remember of the place were the golden lanterns strung from the ceiling, the green matchbooks with gold lanterns embossed on the cover, the steamy, bustling kitchen where we kids were not allowed, and the dark storeroom where we spent hours rolling around on a dolly and climbing up boxes stacked almost ceiling-high. I enjoyed the summer trips to Sacramento, if only as a departure from the daily existence of Chinatown. Once, we slept in an unairconditioned hotel room and I could hear my brother and sister having a water fight in the bathtub next door as I tossed and turned in bed. Once, we discovered an empty storefront and spent the morning impersonating mannequins to the amusement of passersby.

[9]   The banquets were memorable. Unlike today's banquets where people eat and run, they were all-day family affairs. Cases of Bireley's orange sodas, sparkling cider, Seagrams 7, mounds of *gwa-chi* (melon seeds), candy kisses, coconut candy, were always on hand. In the screened-off area, the men and very often the women gambled and talked loudly, among the din of clacking *mah-jongg* tiles, dominoes and Cantonese opera blaring from the loudspeakers. One elderly woman passed water right in her chair, she was so engrossed in her game! The men liked to drink and make speeches. They toasted from table to table during the nine-course banquet, ignoring their wives' worried glances.

[10]   The Cantonese people that I knew were very different from the Chinese people I read about in newspapers or books. They did not resemble the fawning stereotypes I saw on television or films. The Cantonese I had grown up with were vibrant, adventurous, passionate, courageous, proud, and fiercely loyal family men and women. The men were given to bouts of drinking and gambling, often as their sole escape from a lifestyle of virtual exile. The women embraced their rituals and superstitions as a talisman against harm, appeasing the gods with chicken and wine on Chinese New Year's Day, consulting soothsayers and oracles from yarrow stalks and chanting to ward off evil spirits.

[11]   I am sitting in Mrs. Wong's living room in the town of Locke, which is near Sacramento, and am looking up at her wallful of memories—children, grandchildren, husband, young wife . . . I am touched with sadness. I want to bring her oranges once a month, sit and chat with her about the size and brilliant color of her *gwa*, her infallible fishing technique, her expert knitting which she proudly holds up for my inspection. A white vest for her only son who lives in Sacramento with his family. I do not ask how often he comes because I know it is not often enough.

[12]   I become that son, sharing in his guilt. I am that generation of Chinese-American who fled the Chinatowns. The invisible breed. The shamed, who, like the Jews, bury the scars of the diaspora; but unlike the Jews, we cannot escape our yellow skins behind masks of white.

[13]   She brings me an ice-cold 7-Up. I am not thirsty, but I graciously accept. It is safe here, better than the city. I think about my mother wandering like a frightened child in the darkness; my thoughtlessness had sent her unknowingly into the new underground metro-muni subway. The train never emerged from the tunnel and she could not read the English signs. She could not even return to her departure point because the train had switched routes at the end of the line. Mother wandered the length of the city, looking for a familiar Chinese face, any face.

[14]   It does not matter that my mother and Mrs. Wong have been in this country a majority of their lives. Their lot as Chinese women had been circumscribed, preordained here as it was in China, except that now there was no need for bound feet. Like mother, Mrs. Wong has never learned to speak English. Life in Locke and other American Chinatowns was self-sufficient, insular. You toiled in the fields, orchards, factories, sweatshops, and came home at night to your own teacup, bowl of rice, and four walls. There was a curtain that hid you from the outer world. . . .

****

[15]   "You hold his hand right now!" the white kindergarten teacher scolded, as the children filed out in pairs for recess. How could I explain to her what the other Chinese children had told me—that skin color was transferable. If I held the negro boy's hand, I too would turn as dark as a *see-you-guy* (soy-sauce chicken). Deep within, I sensed my attitude was perverse, yet I still spent the remainder of recess in the lavatory, scrubbing the ubiquitous mark of Cain, which the Mormon missionaries who came to Chinatown spoke about, from my palm.

[16]   I used to hide my lunches from the other kids because they laughed at my *joong* (sweet rice with a duck-egg yolk, pork and peanut filling, boiled into a glutinous lump wrapped in banana leaves), or they would wrinkle their noses in disgust at my greasy deep-fried Chinese New Year's dumplings and other

such incriminating un-American concoctions. Being Chinese in America always seemed a liability to me until much later in my youth when I realized the lack of any identifying American culture.

[17]   Before father died, I tried to convey to him the importance of reclaiming our Chinese-American history. My father, like so many of his first generation cohorts, however, always felt that what history was lost was not worth retrieving. "What's the use?" he used to say with a helpless shrug. Years later, as I talked to an old man in Locke, I was to hear the same words repeated over and over. *"Mo-yoong, mo-yoong . . . ,"* he kept repeating bitterly. "It's no use, it's no use . . ." He tells me his family was slaughtered in the war (Sino-Japanese), and blinks back tears. "Nobody's left here," he says, gesturing around the crumbling wooden house with an age-peppered hand. *"Mo-yoong-ah . . .* And I'm too old."

****

[18]   I dreamt father was alive. I nuzzled against him the way I did as a small child, and felt his warmth. The hands that held me were smooth, gentle, unlike the tensed veins that stood on the back of his hands and the tapered fingers that tapped nervous rhythms on tabletops, the calloused palms once swollen white with pus and sores from beating flames out of my hair and clothes when the sash of my dress caught in the open gas fireplace while thumbing through the pages of a Montgomery Ward catalog (my favorite pastime).

[19]   Like watching a fading dinosaur, I watched father's strength give way to age. This handsome, worldly, natty *gum-san-hock,* this guest of the Gold Mountain with the impish grin, who once boasted he owned the first LaSalle in Chinatown; the Arthur Murray dance expert who could rhumba, swing, and out-fox-trot any *bok-guey* (white demon) since Fred Astaire; the droll Chinese Jack Benny who refused to age beyond his long-past thirty-nine years; the hot-tempered septuagenarian who bellowed Cantonese opera around the house and who once challenged a rude young clansman less than half his age to a fight for turning down the Cantonese music during a banquet—had become the inevitable victim of a dying breed.

[20]   The twinkle in his eyes disappeared into two cloudy cataracts and soon into two distant gray moons blinking behind Coke-bottle thick lenses. I saw the once quick, reptilian grace slow to measured, halting steps intermittently punctuated by coughs and breathlessness. But most frightening of all, I saw him sleeping corpselike but still breathing in the winter before his death. My four-year-old daughter whispered as we peeked into his room, "Is *Gung-Gung* (grandfather) going to die?" I hushed her and quickly closed the door.

[21]   Father came to *Gum-San* three times in his lifetime. He came as a young boy with grandfather. He returned at sixteen to China, then came back. It was on his third trip to China that he married mother. He lived with her in *Chel-kai* for four and a half years before coming back to the States for the last time.

[22]   He always threatened that when I turned eighteen he was going to return to China. Then his duties as husband and father would have been fulfilled. Like many of his kinsmen, however, the communist takeover in China destroyed the dream of retiring in wealth to their native villages.

****

[23]   It has taken me many years to reconcile my father's pain with my father's pride. I remember as a little girl holding my big Poppa's hand as we walked into his sewing shop on Powell and Vallejo. We were greeted by the hostile presence of a towering redheaded white lady. She stormed at him, "Mr. Lim, if you do not finish this lot by next Wednesday, I'm going to give the next shipment to another Chinaman, is that clear?"

[24]   I remember how I waited with anxious anticipation for my fearless father to tell that ugly old white lady to shut up and then hit her. I remember how stunned and confused I was when my father did nothing; instead, head bowed, he answered under his breath, "OK, Ci-Ci."

[25]   I feel rage spilling into me as I think of how on that day Ci-Ci towered above us like a redhaired ghost, reducing my beautiful, shining, mythological father into an insignificant Chinaman.

[26]   That was twenty-five years ago. I have not had to make such compromises in my life, thanks to my father. His legacy of sweat and hard work has left me with a richer life and is still very much alive. It is the Cantonese opera. I hear it in my sleep, in my dreams. It awakens that part of me which lies buried deep along the Pacific route to America decades before I was born. I can sing it perfectly in my sleep. The Cantonese flows out of my lips like the Pearl River.

[27]   I might have been a diva in China. It used to frustrate me that the moment I awakened the language would be lost. Now I see the loss can be taken as a gain. The trick is to render the opera in English when I awake. In spite of what the critics and skeptics say, I know it can be done. It's like learning a whole new language. I rather like my *juk-sing* phrasing. Who says a hollow bamboo can't sing?

Source: Gary Soto (Ed.) (1988). *California childhood: Recollections and stories from the golden state* (pp. 33–38). Berkeley, CA: Creative Arts Book Company.

TASK 15: Answer the following questions. Discuss your answers in a small group or with a partner.

1. Where was Genny Lim raised?

2. Why is Genny surprised to be singing Cantonese opera in her dream? What is the significance of the dream?

3. What languages does Genny speak?

4. What did Genny's father do for a living?

5. What kind of experiences did Genny have at school?

6. How did Genny feel about her father?

7. Describe Genny's father physically.

APPLYING THE CONCEPTS

As a second-generation Chinese-American, Genny admires much about Chinese culture, practices, and values. She also finds some aspects of Chinese culture that "collide" or conflict with American culture.

TASK 16: Based on your reading of "A *Juk-Sing* Opera," make two lists of information in the grid below.

ASPECTS OF CHINESE CULTURE THAT GENNY ADMIRES	ASPECTS OF CHINESE CULTURE THAT COLLIDE WITH AMERICAN CULTURE

TASK 17: Below are three quotations from "A *Juk-Sing* Opera." Locate each quotation in the story and determine its meaning. What does each quotation show us about the degree of assimilation that immigrants and their children exhibit? The first one has been done for you.

1. "I am that generation of Chinese-American who fled the Chinatowns. The invisible breed. The shamed, who, like the Jews, bury the scars of the diaspora; but unlike the Jews, we cannot escape our yellow skins behind masks of white."

Meaning in the story: Genny says this as she sits in the living room of an older

Chinese woman, Mrs. Wong. Mrs. Wong maintains her Chinese customs and lives as

a Chinese in the U.S. She has one son, who never comes to visit her. When she says

"I am that generation of Chinese-American who fled the Chinatowns," she is
comparing herself to Mrs. Wong's son. She is saying that she has abandoned her
Chinese culture. She is ashamed of being Chinese and of being an immigrant. She
compares herself and all children of Chinese immigrants to the Jews who
immigrated all over the world. The only difference is that Chinese immigrants
cannot blend in to American society easily because of their skin color.

Degree of assimilation: _First-generation immigrants, like Mrs. Wong, usually_
maintain the culture and values from their homeland. Their children, however,
abandon their cultural heritage. In fact, sometimes they are even ashamed of their
background. They adopt American culture and values to try to blend in with the
dominant religious and ethnic groups. For Chinese immigrants and others, this can
be very difficult because they come from a different ethnic group and cannot easily
blend into the white American culture.

2. " . . . I heard people call my father 'Chinaman.' Yet, his erect, proud bearing never
   betrayed any anger or humiliation. And I now realize the alienation that pride cost
   him."

   Meaning in the story: _____

   _____

   _____

   _____

   Degree of assimilation: _____

   _____

   _____

   _____

3. "His [my father's] legacy of sweat and hard work has left me with a richer life and is
   still very much alive."

   Meaning in the story: _____

   _____

   _____

   _____

   Degree of assimilation: _____

   _____

   _____

   _____

TASK 18: What do Genny Lim's experiences and feelings teach us about the different assimilation models: total assimilation, the melting pot, cultural pluralism, and triple generation theory? Give examples from the text to support your thinking. The first one has been done as an example.

1. Total assimilation:

Genny Lim's mother doesn't exhibit any characteristics of total assimilation. She only speaks Chinese and rarely leaves her Chinese neighborhood.

2. The melting pot:

_____

_____

_____

3. Cultural pluralism:

_____

_____

_____

4. The triple generation theory:

_____

_____

_____

EVALUATING THROUGH WRITING

One of the pleasures of reading literature is to make connections between characters in the story and ourselves and people we know. In "A *Juk-Sing* Opera," Genny Lim has very fond memories of her father.

TASK 19: Think about your childhood, your family, and favorite people from your past. Choose one of the topics below and write a journal entry about it.

1. Describe a distinctive childhood memory that involves a favorite relative.
2. Describe a special relationship with an older person.
3. Describe an unusual dream that may be significant or may connect you with your past.

Task 20: Choose one of the two writing tasks outlined below and write a formal academic essay about the topic. Consult the Academic Strategy box below to learn how to apply a theoretical model to a real-world or literary example.

1. Interview someone with an immigrant history. Ask this person to tell you about his/her family's immigration experience. Go back to the questions you wrote in Task 11 to prepare yourself for the interview. Use any questions that you might find helpful. Here are some additional questions you might ask:

   • Which generation and family members first came to the host country?
   • When did they come?
   • Where did they come from and where did they settle?
   • What was their life in the host country like in the early years?
   • What problems, if any, did they encounter?

   To develop your essay, use the answers to these questions. Decide which model of assimilation this family's immigration experience conforms to. Support your ideas with this family's immigration experience.

2. In "A *Juk-Sing* Opera," Genny Lim discusses the experiences and problems with assimilating into American culture experienced by a second-generation Chinese-American and her father, the person who originally immigrated to the United States. Which model of assimilation does the immigration experience of Genny Lim's family conform to? To develop your essay, use the ideas and quotations from the story.

ACADEMIC STRATEGY: APPLYING A THEORETICAL MODEL TO EXAMPLES

The writing tasks above require that you select one of four theoretical models or frameworks and apply it to an example—either the literary example of Genny Lim's family or the example of the individual you interviewed. Applying a theoretical model is one of the most powerful tools a writer can use to explain behavior or events.

The steps below, as illustrated by the example of Ingrid Jensen's family, are useful ones to follow:

• Provide the background information and thesis statement.

Ingrid Jensen was born in Los Angeles in 1952. Her parents moved there from Wisconsin before Ingrid was born. Although Ingrid's parents were both born in the United States, their parents (Ingrid's grandparents) were from Denmark. Ingrid's grandparents spoke only Danish at home; however, Ingrid's father speaks English and can understand only limited Danish. Ingrid's mother can still speak Danish, but speaks to her children only in English. Despite their Danish heritage, Ingrid's parents have never been to Denmark; Ingrid has traveled to Denmark to meet some of her relatives, and is currently studying Danish in the evenings. Because each generation has its distinct characteristics, Ingrid's family illustrates the triple generation theory.

• Divide the model into its component parts. These parts will suggest an organization for the entire essay.

The triple generation theory is divided into three parts. The first generation are the newly arrived immigrants who maintain an Old World orientation. The second generation are their children, who are born in the host country and adopt a New

World orientation. The third generation are the children of the second generation, who are interested in their ethnic heritage.

- Connect the framework with the examples, and elaborate on this connection.

Ingrid's grandparents represent the first generation. They immigrated to the United States from Denmark. They maintained their Old World orientation by continuing Danish customs and speaking Danish as their primary language. In fact, none of them spoke English fluently. Their children, Ingrid's parents, are examples of the second generation. They were born in the United States and speak English as their primary language. They have a New World orientation and know very little about Danish customs and language, although Ingrid's mother speaks Danish. Ingrid is the third generation. She, like her parents, has a New World orientation but she is very interested in connecting to her Danish roots, as shown by the fact that she has traveled to Denmark and studied Danish.

- Conclude the essay by summarizing or reiterating the essay's main idea. The conclusion should clearly demonstrate the connection between the theoretical model and the example.

The triple generation theory takes into account differences in assimilation patterns across generations and over time. In the case of the Jensen family history, the first generation doesn't truly assimilate. The second generation is fully assimilated, and the third generation looks nostalgically at family roots and ethnic heritage. Thus the triple generation-theory helps us to better understand the Jensen family and others like it in terms of patterns of assimilation over three generations.

TASK 21: Read the following first draft, which was written by a student in response to Question 2 in Task 20. Use the peer feedback form on page 140 to comment on this draft. On a separate piece of paper, respond to the questions. Be clear and specific in the feedback you provide. Compare your comments with those of two of your classmates.

Draft: From "A *Juk-Sing* Opera"

by D.K.

Genny Lim's family is an immigrant family which represents the generational gap in the process of immigration. Her father, conforming to much of the cultural pluralism theory, is shown as a typical first generation immigrant who rarely practice the needs of assimilation. On paragraph 6, Genny writes, "Because of his need for the secure kinship of fellow villagers, father never left Chinatown." We do not really know what this need really is, whether it was manifested internally or externally. By staying in his Chinatown, he was creating himself as a member of cultural pluralism. It may still be found in near town such as Koreatown where Koreans tend to stay together in a town and having a business with their own people. The conditions of living might differ from the Genny's father, but these Koreans hold intimate relationships with themselves rather than other ethnicities. It is because it's convenient for them, and this convenience comes from the cultural background. Personally, I understand their positions but they also need to acknowledge the importance of the assimilation process.

On the other hand, Genny stands more to the triple generation theory since she shows some mixtures of old and new cultures. In paragraph 5, a well descriptive sentence states that "As a second generation American born Chinese, I was often a living contradiction of dual values and identities." Also, throughout the stories she brings out her experiences in the early school years which gave her more contradictions. She was an American while being a Chinese, and her experiences conform to the triple generation theory which deals with the levels of assimilation among different generations. Genny's contradiction, on the other side, is a product of society or to speak host-country's language as often they speak their own language. It may be inappropriate for the immigrant group to insist their own cultures while living in a host-country.

But the harmonization is also possible. People may find themselves being assimilated to a host-culture, and at the same time retaining their own cultures. If this could be attained, we may be in a better position in appreciating the cultural diversities.

Good writing is the result of feedback and revision. Not only can students improve their draft by getting feedback from their instructors, but they can also benefit from *peer feedback,* or comments from their classmates. Effective feedback should include comments on content, organization, and language. When providing feedback, you should make constructive comments, giving concrete suggestions that will be useful for the writer during the revision process. To write constructive comments:

ACADEMIC STRATEGY

USING PEER FEEDBACK TO REVISE ACADEMIC ESSAYS

- Read the entire paper before commenting.
- Begin with a positive comment.
- Be specific, especially when making suggestions for improvement.
- Comment selectively (e.g., on patterns of language errors or on word choice that interferes with comprehension).

Peer Feedback Form

CONTENT

1. What is the writer's main idea and how does he or she support it?
2. How does the writer incorporate information from the story and the academic sources?
3. What background information does the writer provide?
4. Does the writer incorporate any of his or her own ideas or experiences in the essay?
5. What suggestions do you have for the writer to improve the content of this essay?

ORGANIZATION

1. What pattern of organization does the writer use and how effective is this pattern overall?
2. How does the writer introduce the topic?
3. How does the writer conclude the essay?
4. What suggestions do you have for the writer to improve the organization of this essay?

LANGUAGE

1. Does the writer incorporate quotes and/or ideas from the source text(s) correctly?
2. Are there any subject-verb agreement errors in this essay?
3. Are there any word-choice errors in this essay?
4. List any other language errors.
5. What suggestions do you have for the writer to improve the language of this essay?

TASK 22: Ask a classmate to use the peer feedback form to review and critique the first draft of the essay you wrote for Task 20. Use this feedback to revise your draft.

INSIGHTS FROM ANTHROPOLOGY

INTRODUCTION:
IMAGES OF FAMILY LIFE

Cultural anthropologists have found that families exist in every culture. However, families are defined and structured in a variety of forms to fill social, economic, and political needs. Understanding family patterns, structures, and relationships is an integral part of the study of cultural anthropology. In this chapter, definitions of the family unit are explored from multiple perspectives.

Exploring the Concepts

EXPLORING THROUGH VISUAL IMAGES

Families come in all sizes and configurations. Anthropologists have found wide variations in the family unit, even within large cultural groups such as those found in the United States.

TASK 1: Look at the family photos on the next page. Discuss what you might infer about each family in terms of such characteristics as their cultural background, social class, etc.

✪ Targeting Grammar: Using Modals to Express Possibility

Modals are auxiliary verbs that do not change forms. The modals *must, could, might,* and *may* express degrees of possibility in affirmative and negative sentences:

AFFIRMATIVE EXAMPLES	DEGREE OF POSSIBILITY
The woman in the center **is** my mother. (present tense, no modal)	fact: 100 percent certain
The old man in the photograph **must be** the grandfather.	strong possibility
Could that young woman **be** the daughter of that man?	weak possibility
The small boy **might be** the son of the woman—I'm not sure.	weak possibility
The young girl **may be** the sister of the little boy.	weak possibility

In negative sentences, the uses change slightly:

NEGATIVE EXAMPLES	DEGREE OF POSSIBILITY
The older man on the left **isn't** related to me at all. (present tense, no modal)	fact: 100 percent certain
Joe's little boy has red hair—he **must not be** his son.	strong possibility
They look totally different—they **couldn't be** sisters!	strong possibility
That **can't be** her mother—she looks too young.	strong possibility
The people pictured here **might not** even **be** alive anymore—we haven't spoken to that side of the family for years.	weak possibility

TASK 2: Use modal expressions of possibility to describe the relationships of the individuals in the photos. Work in pairs or in small groups.

🌀 Targeting Vocabulary: Kinship Terms

TASK 3: Fill in the family tree below with the terms from the list. Note that some of the terms may be used more than once. Then, with a partner, compare your answers.

mother ⎱ daughter ⎰ maternal grandmother
      ⎰ sister ⎱ maternal grandfather   ⎱ maternal great-grandparents ⎰   uncle   first cousin   great-uncle

father ⎱ son ⎰ paternal grandmother   aunt   second cousin   great-aunt
      ⎰ brother ⎱ paternal grandfather   ⎱ paternal great-grandparents ⎰

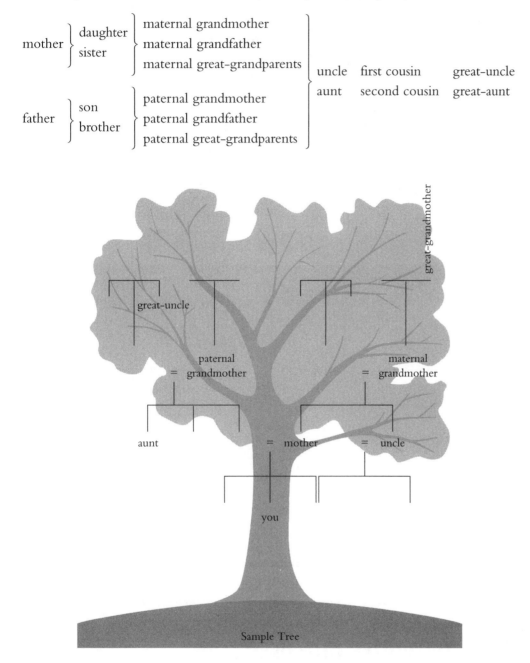

Sample Tree

TASK 4: On separate paper, draw your family tree. How many generations can you label? Share your tree with two classmates, explaining the family relationships.

EXPLORING THROUGH WRITING

TASK 5: What constitutes a family? Explore this question by writing a journal entry.

Marriage

Gary Ferraro

Marriage and the Family: A Definition

[1]   The family is distinct from the institution of marriage, which is defined as a series of customs formalizing the relationship between male and female adults within the family. Marriage is a socially approved union between a man and a woman that regulates the sexual and economic rights and obligations between them. Marriage usually involves an explicit contract or understanding and is entered into with the assumption that it will be a permanent arrangement.

Sexual Union

[2]   As with any term, the definition of marriage frequently must be qualified. Marriage, according to our definition, is a socially legitimate sexual union. When a man and a woman are married, it is implied that they are having a sexual relationship—or that the society permits them to have one should they desire it. Although this is generally true, we should bear in mind that this social legitimacy is not absolute, for there may be specified periods during which sexual relations with one's spouse may be taboo.

Permanence

[3]   A second qualification to our definition relates to the permanence of the marital union. Frequently, as part of the marriage vows recited in Western weddings, spouses pledge to live together in matrimony "until death do us part." Even though it is difficult to ascertain a person's precise intentions or expectations when entering a marriage, an abundance of data suggests that the permanence of marriage varies widely, and in no societies do all marriages last until death. Recent statistics, for example, indicate that more than one of every two marriages in the United States ends in divorce. Relatively impermanent marriages can also be found in smaller-scale societies.

Common Residence

[4]   A qualifying statement must also be added about the notion that family members share a common residence. Although, by and large, family members do live together, there are some obvious definitional problems. If we define "sharing a common residence" as living under the same roof, a long list of exceptions can be cited. In Western society, dependent children sometimes live away from home at boarding schools and colleges. Additionally, in this age of high-speed transportation and communication, it is possible for a husband and wife to live and work in two different cities and see each other only on weekends. On a more global scale, 94 of the 240 African societies listed in Murdock's *Ethnographic Atlas* (1967) are characterized by wives and their children living in separate houses from the husband. In some non-Western societies, adolescent boys live with their peers apart from their families; and in some cases, such as the Nyakyusa (Wilson 1960), adolescent boys have not only their own houses but indeed their own villages. In each of these examples, family membership and participation are not dependent upon living under the same roof.

[5]   Thus, as we are beginning to see, the terms *marriage* and *family* are not easy to define. For years, anthropologists have attempted to arrive at definitions of these terms that will cover all known societies. Frequently, anthropologists have debated whether or not families and the institution of marriage are universals.

Marriage and the Family: Functions

[6]   Whether or not marriage is a cultural universal found in all societies depends, of course, on the level of abstraction in our definitions. Without entering into that debate here, suffice it to say that the formation of families through marriage serves several important functions for the societies in which the families operate. One social benefit that marriage provides is the creation of relatively stable relationships between men and women that regulate sexual mating and reproduction. Since humans are continually sexually receptive and (in the absence of contraceptives) sexual activity usually leads to reproduction, it is imperative that societies create and maintain relatively permanent unions that will regulate mating, reproduction, and child rearing in a socially approved manner.

[7]   A second social benefit of marriage is that it provides a mechanism for regulating the sexual division of labor that exists to some extent in all societies. For reasons that are both biological and cultural, men in all societies perform some tasks, while women perform others. To maximize the chances of survival, it is important for a society to arrange the exchange of goods and services between men and women. Marriage usually brings about domestic relationships that facilitate the exchange of these goods and services.

[8]   Third, marriage creates a set of family relationships that can provide for the material, educational, and emotional needs of children for a relatively long period of time. Unlike most other animal species, human children are dependent on adults for the first decade or more of their lives for their nourishment, shelter, and protection. Moreover, human children

require adults to provide the many years of cultural learning needed to develop into fully functioning members of the society. Even though it is possible for children to be reared largely outside a family (as is done on the kibbutzim of Israel), in most societies marriage creates a set of family relationships that provide the material, educational, and emotional support children need for their eventual maturity.

Source: (1995). *Cultural anthropology: An applied perspective* (2nd ed.) (pp. 196–198). New York: West Publishing Company.

TASK 8: Skim the text to locate the paragraph in which each main idea below is found and write its paragraph number in the space provided. Then read each statement to determine if the sentence discusses the *definition* of marriage or its *functions* and write this in the blank provided. The first one is done for you.

¶ _8_ 1. Marriage creates a set of family relationships that can provide for the material, educational, and emotional needs of children for a relatively long period of time.   _function_

¶ ___ 2. A second qualification to our definition relates to the permanence of the marital union.   _____

¶ ___ 3. In each of these examples, family membership and participation are not dependent upon living under the same roof.   _____

¶ ___ 4. Marriage is a socially approved union between a man and a woman that regulates the sexual and economic rights and obligations between them.   _____

¶ ___ 5. Marriage provides the creation of relatively stable relationships between men and women that regulate sexual mating and reproduction.   _____

¶ ___ 6. Suffice it to say that the formation of families through marriage serves several important functions for the societies in which the families operate.   _____

¶ ___ 7. Marriage usually brings about domestic relationships that facilitate the exchange of goods and services between men and women.   _____

¶ ___ 8. Marriage, according to our definition, is a socially legitimate sexual union.   _____

⊚ Targeting Grammar: Qualifying a Definition with Subordinators

To narrow or qualify the definitions of academic terms, writers often follow general definitions with statements that begin with subordinators such as *(al)though* or *even though*. Study the following examples from "Marriage":

DEFINITION		QUALIFICATION
The definition of marriage must be qualified. Marriage, according to our definition, is a socially legitimate sexual union.	+	**Although** this is generally true, we should bear in mind that this social legitimacy is not absolute, for there may be specified periods during which sexual relations with one's spouse may be taboo.
A second qualification to our definition relates to the permanence of the marital union.	+	**Even though** it is difficult to ascertain a person's precise intentions or expectations when entering a marriage, an abundance of data suggests that the permanence of marriage varies widely, and in no societies do all marriages last until death.
A qualifying statement must also be added about the notion that family members share a common residence.	+	**Although,** by and large, family members do live together, there are some obvious definitional problems. **If** we define "sharing a common residence" as living under the same roof, a long list of exceptions can be cited.

TASK 9: Reread "Romantic Love" in Task 3. Based on the information contained in the reading, write a definition of romantic love. Your definition should consist of at least two sentences and contain a subordinator such as *although* or *even though*. Compare your definition with those of your classmates. How are your definitions different?

UNDERSTANDING THROUGH LISTENING

VIDEO

> **Lecture:** Kinship and Marriage
> **Segment 4:** Marriage Partners
>
> **Professor:** Nancy Levine
> **Course:** Anthropology 9: Cultural Anthropology
> **Text:** *Cultural Anthropology: An Applied Perspective* by Gary Ferraro

In this lecture segment, Professor Levine discusses kinship and cultural views of permissible marriage partners.

TASK 10: Before watching Professor Levine's lecture, study the terms below. Put a check mark (√) next to the terms you are unfamiliar with. Then as you view the lecture, take notes and try to determine the meanings of these key terms.

_____ brother/sister marriage   _____ incest taboo

_____ cross cousins   _____ parallel cousins

_____ first cousin   _____ royal families

_____ genetic repercussions   _____ same-sex sibling

_____ genetically deleterious   _____ spouse

TASK 11: Watch the lecture again and, from your notes, write a brief definition for each term in the space provided. Then work in small groups to compare your definitions. The first one has been done for you.

KEY TERM	DEFINITION
1. brother/sister marriage	Preferred form of marriage in Egypt during Roman times; brother and sister marry to keep inheritance.
2. cross cousins	
3. first cousin	
4. genetic repercussions	
5. genetically deleterious	
6. incest taboo	
7. parallel cousins	
8. royal families	
9. same-sex sibling	
10. spouse	

UNDERSTANDING THROUGH READING 2

In "Mate Selection," the author describes how different cultures determine whom you can and cannot marry.

TASK 12: Scan "Mate Selection" for the subheadings and write them in the left-hand column below. Then write your prediction about the content of each section in the right-hand column. The first one has been done for you.

HEADING/SUBHEADINGS	PREDICTION
1. Mate Selection: Whom Should You Marry?	1. Who should marry whom; who decides?
2.	2.
3.	3.
4.	4.

TASK 13: As you read "Mate Selection," see if your predictions are accurate.

MATE SELECTION

Gary Ferraro

Mate Selection: Whom Should You Marry?

[1]   Every society known to anthropology has established for itself some type of rules regulating mating (sexual intercourse). The most common form of prohibition is mating with certain types of kin who are defined by the society as being inappropriate sexual partners. These prohibitions on mating with certain categories of relatives are known as *incest taboos.* Following the lead of Fox (1967:54–55), it is important to distinguish between sexual relationship and marriage. Incest taboos refer to prohibitions against having sexual relations with certain categories of kin. This is not exactly the same thing as rules prohibiting marrying certain kin. Although incest taboos and rules prohibiting marrying certain kin often coincide with each other (that is, those who are forbidden to have sex are also forbidden to marry), it cannot be assumed that they do in fact coincide.

[2]   As we have seen, every society has the notion of incest that defines a set of kin with whom a person is to avoid marriage and sexual intimacy. In no society is it permissible to mate with one's parents or siblings (i.e., within the nuclear family), and in most cases the restricted group of kin is considerably wider. Beyond this notion of incest, people in all societies are faced with rules either restricting one's choice of marriage partners or strongly encouraging the selection of other people as highly desirable mates. These are known as rules of *exogamy* (marrying outside of a certain group) and *endogamy* (marrying within a certain group).

Rules of Exogamy

[3]   Owing to the universality of the incest taboo, all societies to one degree or another have rules for marrying outside a certain group of kin. These are known as rules of exogamy. In societies like the United States, which are not based on the principle of unilineal descent groups, the exogamous group extends only slightly beyond the nuclear family. It is considered either illegal or immoral to marry one's first cousin and, in some cases, one's second cousin, but beyond that one can marry other distant relatives with only mild disapproval. In societies that are based on unilateral descent groups, however, the exogamous group is

usually the lineage, which can include many hundreds of people, or even the clan, which can include thousands of people who are unmarriageable. Thus, when viewed cross-culturally, rules of exogamy based on kinship do not appear to be based on genealogical proximity.

Rules of Endogamy

[4]   In contrast to exogamy, which requires marriage *outside* one's own group, the rule of endogamy requires a person to select a mate from *within* one's own group. Hindu castes found in traditional India are strongly endogamous, believing that to marry below one's caste would result in serious ritual pollution. Caste endogamy is also found in a somewhat less rigid form among the Rwanda and Banyankole of eastern Central Africa. In addition to being applied to caste, endogamy can be applied to other social units, such as the village or local community, as was the case among the Incas of Peru, or to racial groups, as has been practiced in the Republic of South Africa for much of the present century.

[5]   Even though there are no strongly sanctioned rules of endogamy in the United States, there is a certain amount of marrying within one's own groups based on class, ethnicity, religion, and race. This general de facto endogamy found in the United States results from the fact that people do not have frequent social contacts with people from different backgrounds. Upper-middle-class children, for example, tend to grow up in the suburbs, take golf and tennis lessons at the country club, and attend schools designed to prepare students for college. By contrast, many lower-class children grow up in urban housing projects, play basketball in public playgrounds, and attend schools with low expectations for college attendance. This general social segregation by class, coupled with parental and peer pressure to "marry your own kind," results in a relatively high level of endogamy in many complex Western societies such as our own.

[6]   It should be noted that rules of exogamy and rules of endogamy are not opposites or mutually exclusive. Indeed, they can coexist in the same society provided the endogamous group is larger than the exogamous group. For example, it is quite possible to have an endogamous ethnic group (i.e., one must marry within one's ethnic group) while at the same time having exogamous lineages (i.e., one must marry outside one's own lineage).

Arranged Marriages

[7]   In Western societies, with their strong emphasis on individualism, mate selection is largely a decision made jointly by the prospective bride and groom. Aimed at satisfying the emotional and sexual needs of the individual, the choice of mates in Western society is based on such factors as physical attractiveness, emotional compatibility, and romantic love. Even though absolute freedom of choice is constrained by such factors as social class, ethnicity, religion and race, individuals in most contemporary Western societies are relatively free to marry whomever they please.

[8]   In many societies, however, the interests of the families are so strong that marriages are arranged. Negotiations are handled by family members of the prospective bride and groom, and for all practical purposes, the decision of whom one will marry is made by one's parents or other influential family members. In certain cultures, such as parts of traditional Japan, India, and China, future marriage partners are betrothed while they are still children. In one extreme example—the Tiwi of North Australia—females are betrothed or promised as future wives *before* they are born (Hart and Pilling 1960:14). Since the Tiwi believe that females are liable to become impregnated by spirits at any time, the only sensible precaution against unmarried mothers is to betroth female babies before birth or as soon as they are born.

[9]   All such cases of *arranged marriages,* wherever they may be found, are based on the cultural assumption that since marriage is a union of two kin groups rather than merely two individuals, it is far too significant an institution to be based on something as frivolous as physical attractiveness or romantic love.

[10]   Arranged marriages are frequently found in societies with elaborate social hierarchies, perhaps the best example of which is Hindu India. Indeed, the maintenance of the caste system in India is dependent, by and large, upon a system of arranged marriages. As Goode reminds us:

> Maintenance of caste was too important a matter to be left to the young, who might well fall prey to the temptations of love and thus ignore caste requirements. To prevent any serious opposition, youngsters were married early enough to ensure that they could not acquire any resources with which to oppose adult decisions. The joint family, in turn, offered an organization which could absorb a young couple who could not yet make their own living . . . . This pattern of marriage has always been common among the nobility, but in India it developed not only among the wealthy, who could afford early marriages and whose unions might mark an alliance between two families, but also among the poor, who had nothing to share but their debts. (1963:208)

[11]   Arranged marriages in India are further reinforced by other traditional Indian values. Fathers, it was traditionally held, sinned by failing to marry off their daughters before puberty. Indeed, both parents in

India shared the common belief that they were responsible for any sin the daughter might commit because of a late marriage. For centuries, Hindu civilization, with its heritage of eroticism expressed in the sexual cult of Tantricism, has viewed women as lustful beings who tempt men with their sexual favors. Thus, a girl had to be married at an early age to protect both herself and those men who might become sinners. And if females were to become brides before reaching adolescence, they could hardly be trusted to select their own husbands.

Source: (1995). *Cultural anthropology: An applied perspective* (2nd ed.) (pp. 198–202). New York: West Publishing Company.

TASK 14: Check the predictions you made in Task 12 against what you have learned from the reading. Below, list three new facts you learned about marriage rules in different cultures.

1. _____

_____

2. _____

_____

3. _____

_____

TASK 15: Within a given culture, marriage rules and taboos serve a purpose such as preserving land or money, strengthening kinship ties, etc. For each of the marital restrictions below, scan the reading again to locate the purpose of the restriction and write it in the space provided. Use your own words. The first one has been done as an example.

RESTRICTION	PURPOSE
1. Incest taboos	1. The purpose of this taboo is to prevent individuals from having sexual relations within certain categories of kin.
2. Rules of exogamy	2.
3. Rules of endogamy	3.
4. Arranged marriages	4.

Integrating Perspectives

ANALYZING THROUGH DISCUSSION

Popular opinion can offer much insight into cultural views and beliefs.

TASK 16: To explore attitudes toward marriage and mate selection, develop a survey to be administered outside of class. Working with a partner or in small groups, create a list of questions to discover how other people feel about the institution of marriage. Here are some possible questions:

- Why do people marry?
- Should everyone get married?
- Should parents or other family members determine whom you marry?
- Should marriage last until death?
- Should people marry for love or economic stability?
- What are the benefits and the costs of marriage?

TASK 17: Administer the survey to three people. Try to find people that you think will have different points of view. Be sure to take notes on their responses.

TASK 18: Compare your survey results with those of the other members of your group. Work together to create an overall compilation of your results. What have you learned about popular attitudes about marriage?

EVALUATING THROUGH LITERATURE

This excerpt from *The Bird Artist* presents a humorous view of arranged marriage in the early twentieth century in an isolated area of Newfoundland, now a province of Canada. The sections below show the progression of this arranged marriage from the first suggestion of the marriage to the actual ceremony.

TASK 19: As you read, focus on the author's view of arranged marriage. How does the author find humor in an arranged marriage?

THE BIRD ARTIST

Howard Norman

[1]   The next thing I was conscious of were the words "Knock, knock," which is what my mother usually said after she had knocked on my door. I had fallen asleep with the photograph face down on my chest. My mother looked pleased. I quickly set it upright on the table.

[2]   "The picture is of your fourth cousin," she said. "Her name—dear thing—is Cora Holly, of Czechoslovakian descent, like your father. She's a cousin on Orkney's side, by way of England. She lives in Richibucto, New Brunswick, a coastal village like ours."

[3]   "What's her picture doing here?"

[4]   "I just *knew* you'd ask that. Well, your father and I are interested in her. In your marrying her, more precisely."

[5]   "What?"

[6]   "That Margaret Handle, whom you've been sleeping with. You know what people say, that she's better to visit than marry."

[7]   "What people? You're like someone gossiping with herself."

[8]   "Calm down, Fabian. Think Cora Holly over, will you, darling? All I ask is that you turn your thoughts to her, for my sake, for your father's. And of course eventually for yours. Because it's our understanding that even the lovely face in that photograph hardly does Cora justice."

[9]   "When's the last time you saw this Cora Holly?"

[10]   "I've never seen her."

[11]   "And the father and mother?"

[12]   "Pavel and Klara? Well, let's see. It would be twenty years."

[13]   "And given that, how'd this photograph get here?"

[14]   "Well, Klara and I have been exchanging letters."

[15]   "You've kept it a close secret."

[16]   "When the mail comes in, you look for letters from Mr. Sprague. You don't ask for anything else."

[17]   "True enough."

[18]   "Cora is keen on marrying you as well."

[19]   She closed my door.

****

[20]   Two weeks later, after a supper of cod, soup, and bread, I made coffee for my father and me. "Did you enjoy the potato-leek soup?" my mother said.

[21]   "Well, you noticed I took a second helping, didn't you?" I said.

[22]   "The Hollys, in their most recent letter, mentioned that potato-leek is Cora's very most favorite. I suppose that, in a way, I made potato-leek tonight in Cora's honor."

[23]   "Here's to Cora Holly, then!" my father said, knocking his coffee mug lightly against mine.

[24]   "The idea is that I should marry her because we both like the same soup?" I said.

[25]   "The *idea*," my mother said, "is quite simple. It is that it's intelligent for fiancés at such a distance to develop a bond in advance. And soup is as natural a thing to start with as any."

[26]   "Did the letter say that Cora was *passionate* about potato-leek soup?" I said.

[27]   Without so much as a glance or utterance, my mother left the kitchen.

[28]   My father stared after her. "Marrying a woman you've known all your life," he said, "Margaret, for instance. Now, that *could* turn out badly. To marry your fourth cousin, come in sight unseen from Richibucto, granted, that's the opposite end of the stick. But it's still marriage. Still the same stick. It's your God-given privilege, and the woman's, to choose without fear of the future or the unknown."

****

[29]   "Where is Cora?" my mother said, walking up to Klara first, kissing her cheek, then over to Pavel, and kissing his.

[30]   "You see," Pavel said, "the bride-to-be is using all the water in Halifax, it seems. She's on her third or fourth bath, I've lost count."

[31]   "Why won't she come out?"

[32]   "It may just be a case of matrimonial jitters," Klara said. "I'm quite sure, had there been more time, you and I could have gone into a separate room and told stories of our own wedding days. Perhaps later, in a letter."

[33]   I had not seen Averell Grey step into the room. "Ahem, excuse me. Welcome," he said.

[34]   "Now isn't this nice," Mrs. Hagerforse said. "Justice of the Peace Grey, this is Alaric Vas, Fabian Vas, Klara Holly in the chair, and Pavel Holly."

[35]   "Pleased. And where is Cora Holly?"

[36]   Grey, a slim man of perhaps sixty, had wispy white hair and age spots on his face, so many it was like a map of islands. "I forgot my Bible," he said. "Of course there's one in this good Christian home."

[37]   We heard the sound of splashing behind the door.

[38]   "I'll be direct here," Pavel said. "There was a Bible in the room here, and by some ingenious means our Cora has wedged it so that the door is impossible to open from the outside. That, along with the lock, of course."

[39]   "I'll need a Bible," Grey said. "For the ceremony."

[40]   "I'll see to it," Mrs. Hagerforse said, leaving the room.

[41]   "Fabian," Pavel said, "as her future husband, you might try and convince—"

[42]   "I'd like to look at her," I said. "What I mean is, all I've ever seen of your daughter is the photograph."

[43]   "It was an exact likeness," Pavel said. "A few years back likeness."

[44] "There is a practical side to her coming out of the bath," Grey said. "To have the wedding itself. Nothing more practical than that, eh?" He was the only one who laughed.

[45] "We're getting along so well here," Klara said. "Let's all, except for Fabian, go into one of our rooms, or that lovely sitting room downstairs, and continue to."

[46] And in a moment I stood at the bathroom door, waiting for the spigot to be shut off. When I heard more splashing, I said, "Cora, it's me, Fabian Vas."

[47] "I'm actually dressed," she said. "I've been dressed for more than an hour. I did take a bath, but then got dressed. I've been filling and emptying the bathtub. All done through pipes here. Not like at home."

[48] The door opened and I stepped back. Add the years hence, but Cora looked much as she had in her photograph, except now she had on a high-collared white lace wedding dress. "You're shorter than in my imagination," she said. "Do you look like your father?"

[49] "A little."

[50] "I've never seen him or you in a photograph. Why wasn't one sent?"

[51] "I don't know."

[52] "Take a good look. I was an ugly child. Then, at age thirteen, I was dizzyingly beautiful. That was my father's opinion, my mother's, my neighbors in Richibucto's. I weighed their opinions carefully, then agreed. First I was ugly, though, then quite the opposite. And now I'm aware I contain both. But that doesn't mean I feel average. I've never felt that. No, it's more that I remember being both ugly and beautiful, and hope that one stays and the other doesn't come back. We'll just have to wait and see."

[53] "Sit down, Cora. Please. In that chair, and I'll sit on the other chair."

[54] We sat looking at each other. I stood, walked into the bathroom, poured a glass of water, and handed it to her.

[55] "Thank you." She drank the water, then held the empty glass. "This is the worst moment of my life."

[56] "I don't know anything. I don't know anything, except one thing that's true—"

[57] "One."

[58] "—it's that my mother and father wanted me to get married in the worst way. Not to Margaret Handle, who—"

[59] "I see."

[60] "Did you get to read my mother's letters?"

[61] "I had parts read to me."

****

[62] Cora put her folded hands on the Bible. I put my hands on top of hers. The ceremony was mercifully brief. At the last moment Cora stepped out of her shoes. I could not possibly know why, except that it was her one personal choice in the matter.

[63] Grey said a few words about life from his own experiences, not mine, not Cora's; then we said the vows. "By the powers invested in me—"

[64] "Fabian, you may kiss the bride."

[65] "No, first the rings," Pavel said.

[66] My mother handed me the rings. She had got them from Romeo Gillette. We exchanged rings. They fit perfectly.

[67] "Fabian—"

[68] My lips—or was it Cora's—were dry as paper.

Source: (1994). *The bird artist* (pp. 41–42; 66–67; 183–185; 189). New York: Picador.

TASK 20: For each of the four sections of this excerpt, answer the questions below by summarizing the events in the appropriate section of the grid.

1. What happened?

2. Who was involved?

3. Where did the event take place?

4. When did the event take place?

	SECTION 1	SECTION 2	SECTION 3	SECTION 4
1.				
2.				
3.				
4.				

TASK 21: Answer the following questions, using the text to support your response:

1. Which characters are in favor of the arranged marriage? Why?

_____

_____

2. What evidence is there of Fabian's reaction to the arranged marriage? Cora's?

_____

_____

3. What might be the cause of Fabian's reaction to the arranged marriage?

_____

_____

4. Do you think Fabian and Cora will stay married?

_____

_____

EVALUATING THROUGH DISCUSSION

ACADEMIC STRATEGY: **PREWRITING DEBATE**	In order to prepare for an argumentation essay, an in-class debate is useful. Preparing your side of the debate helps you to strengthen your own arguments; it also allows you to anticipate or predict the opposing team's arguments and formulate your *refutation*, or your attempt to find errors or inaccuracies in the opponent's argument. Refuting the arguments of the opposition strengthens your position and will become an important part of the essay that you write.

- Decide on your position in this debate and form a team with other students who have the same opinion.
- Choose a group captain and a secretary.
- In your teams, brainstorm reasons for your opinion and possible arguments that the opposing team will present.
- Be ready to defend your own arguments and refute those of the opposing team.
- Each person on the team should present one main point. The group captain will summarize the team's point of view.

TASK 22: Debate one of the following questions:

1. Which is better: a marriage based on romantic love or an arranged marriage based on the parents' decision?

2. Should first-cousin marriages be allowed?

3. Once married, do people have a greater obligation to their spouses and children or to their parents?

EVALUATING THROUGH WRITING

In this unit, the concepts of marriage and kinship have been explored from the perspective of cultural anthropology. Read over the summaries, outlines, and definitions you have written of the readings and lectures to review the family, kinship, and marriage theories presented in the unit.

TASK 23: Choose one of the following topics and write an argumentation essay. Refer to the Academic Strategy box on page 185 for tips on organizing your essay. React to the question by using personal experience and knowledge gained from this unit.

1. React to the quote below. Does a person have a greater obligation to his or her family of orientation (i.e., parents, brothers, and sisters) or to his or her family of procreation (i.e., spouse and children)?

Most of us spend our lives in two families in which we have quite different statuses and roles: a *family of orientation,* the one into which we are born as son or daughter, and a *family of procreation,* the one which we create ourselves as father or mother.

Source: Ian Robertson (1989). *Society: A brief introduction* (pp. 247–248). New York: Worth Publishers, Inc.

---

2. The divorce rate in the United States, where marriages are most often based on romantic love, has increased dramatically over the last fifty years and is now at approximately 50 percent. Given this high divorce rate, is romantic love a sound reason to marry someone? Argue a position supported by examples from cultural practices that you are familiar with.

3. In some states in the United States, it is permissible to marry a first cousin. In some cultures, it is common practice to marry a first cousin. In other cultures, it is taboo to marry anyone from one's immediate family, including first cousins. In your opinion, is first-cousin marriage desirable or undesirable? What are the stipulations or conditions that you believe should be placed on marriage?

ACADEMIC STRATEGY: ORGANIZING AN ARGUMENTATION ESSAY

When writing an argumentation essay, the task of the writer is to convince the audience of the validity and superiority of his or her position. To do so, organization and structure are very important. One organizational pattern consists of the following elements:

- Introduction
- Background
- Arguments
- Refutation of counterarguments
- Conclusion

Develop these primary elements of an argumentation paper in the following way:

INTRODUCTION
The purpose of the introduction is to engage the reader's interest and clearly state the *thesis*, or main idea, of the essay. The thesis statement should concisely identify the author's position, or stance, on the topic.

BACKGROUND
A background paragraph presents information necessary to understand the issues related to the topic and why the topic is controversial. This paragraph should treat the topic as objectively as possible.

ARGUMENTS
This section of the essay identifies the reasons, usually in order of importance, that support the author's position. It is important to support each reason with examples and details that prove the argument. Unsubstantiated claims should not be used.

REFUTATION OF COUNTERARGUMENTS
The purpose of this section is to demonstrate that the author has examined the issue from both sides and chosen the superior position. To do so, the author should present each counterargument and then *refute,* or disprove, it.

CONCLUSION
To end the essay, the author should summarize the arguments both for and against and reiterate strongly his or her position.

INSIGHTS 1 SKILLS-AT-A-GLANCE

	UNIT 1			UNIT 2			UNIT 3			UNIT 4		
	INTRODUCTION	EXPLORATION	EXPANSION	INTRODUCTION	EXPLORATION	EXPANSION	INTRODUCTION	EXPLORATION	EXPANSION	INTRODUCTION	EXPLORATION	EXPANSION
VOCABULARY	• Describing objects	• Verbs expressing relationships • Expressing significance	• Expressing an opinion • Exemplification	• Expressing wind characteristics	• Geographical terms • Word families	• Finding synonyms or paraphrases • Similes	• Synonyms • Connotation and denotation	• Word families • Synonyms		• Kinship terms • Figurative language • Key terms	• Colloquial language • Latin and Greek roots	
GRAMMAR	• Sequencing adjectives • Fronting adverb phrases	• Using adverbs of frequency to qualify a generalization	• Passive verbs in description • Embedded questions	• Participial phrases • Verb tense in description, narration, and explanation • Expressing contrast through subordination	• Subject-verb agreement with present tense verbs • Adverbs of manner, place, and direction	• Nonrestrictive relative clauses indicating location • Using articles with geographical terms	• Cause/effect	• Brief definitions through relative clauses		• Using modals to express possibility • Referring to sources	• Clarification connectors	• Qualifying a definition with subordinators
ACADEMIC STRATEGY	• Extended definitions • Journal writing	• Coping with unfamiliar words in academic lectures • Highlighting or marking a text • Using examples to make a generalization	• Clarifying a point using examples • Characteristics of thesis statements	• Cubing • Comprehending unstressed words • Sensory description in storytelling	• Previewing illustrations in a text • Previewing an academic text • Predicting the contents of a lecture • Skimming and scanning • Synthesizing information • Studying with a partner	• Supporting a thesis statement	• Clustering • Predicting the contents of a reading	• Graphic organizers • Summarizing	• Applying a theory to a case • Applying a theoretical model to examples • Using peer feedback to revise academic essays	• Reacting to readings	• Chaining • Outlining • Mapping	• Agreeing and disagreeing in class discussions • Prewriting debate • Organizing an argumentation essay

187

Text Credits

"The Children's Room" Reprinted by permission of International Creative Management, Inc. Copyright © 1995 by Kathryn Harrison. First appeared in *The New Yorker.*

Excerpts from "Folk Objects" by Simon J. Bronner, in *Folk Groups and Folklore Genres: An Introduction,* Elliott Oring, ed. Copyright © 1986 by Utah State University Press. Reprinted by permission. All rights reserved.

Excerpts from "Material Folk Culture" chapter in *Introduction to Folklore,* D. C. Laubach. © 1989. Portsmouth, NH: Boynton/Cook. With permission of the author.

"My Navajo Home in Los Angeles," Thomas Whiterock, from *Celebrating Diversity: A Multi-Cultural Reader,* B. Lee Brandon, ed. © 1995. Every effort has been made to contact Thomas Whiterock, without success. Information about the copyright holders would be appreciated.

"A Navajo Blanket" from *Nature: Poems Old and New* by May Swenson. Copyright © 1994 by the Literary Estate of May Swenson. Reprinted by permission of Houghton Mifflin Co. All rights reserved.

Excerpt from *Animal Dreams* by Barbara Kingsolver. Copyright © 1990 by Barbara Kingsolver. Reprinted by permission of HarperCollins Publishers, Inc.

Excerpt from *The Stone Diaries* by Carol Shields. Copyright © 1993 by Carol Shields. Used by permission of Viking Penguin, a Division of Penguin Books USA, Inc.

"The Jeaning of America" from *Understanding Popular Culture* by J. Fiske, Boston, MA, Unwin Hyman, 1989.

"Relish the Rhône" by Clive Irving. Courtesy Condé Nast Traveler. Copyright © 1996 by Condé Nast Publications. Inc.

"Demon's Gates and Devil's Doors," Mary Reed, Copyright © 1993, in *Weatherwise,* Dec. 1993/Jan. 1994. Reprinted with permission of The Helen Dwight Reid Educational Foundation. Published by Helldref Publications, 1319 18th St. N.W., Washington, DC 20036-1802.

Excerpts from *Essentials of Meteorology: An Introduction to the Atmosphere* by C. Donald Ahrens. Reprinted by permission. Copyright © 1993 by West Publishing Company. All rights reserved.

"The Wise Man of the Mountains" by Patrick Goldstein. Copyright © 1995 by Patrick Goldstein. By permission of the author.

"Los Angeles Notebook" from *Slouching Towards Bethlehem* by Joan Didion. Copyright © 1968 by Joan Didion. Reprinted by arrangement with Farrar, Straus and Giroux, Inc., New York.

"The New Immigration: 1880–1900" from *The American People: Creating a Nation* by Gary B. Nash and Julie Roy Jeffrey. Copyright © 1994 by HarperCollins College Publishers. Reprinted by permission of Addison-Wesley Educational Publishers, Inc.

Excerpt from *The Huddled Masses: The Immigrant in American Society, 1880–1921* by Alan M. Kraut. Copyright © 1982 by Harlan Davidson, Inc. Reprinted by permission.

Excerpts from *Sociology: A Brief Introduction* by Alex Thio. Copyright © 1991 by HarperCollins College Publishers. Reprinted by permission of Addison-Wesley Educational Publishers, Inc.

Excerpt from *Assimilation in American Life* by M. Gordon. Copyright © 1964 by M. Gordon. Used by permission of Oxford University Press, Inc.

"A *Juk-Sing* Opera" by Genny Lim, from *California Childhood: Recollections and Stories from the Golden State,* Creative Arts Books, Copyright © 1988. Used by permission.

Excerpts from "A Parenting Special Report: The New American Families" in *Parenting,* March 1995. Reprinted by permission of United Feature Syndicate, Inc.

Excerpts from "Why Men Need Family Values" by Robert G. Samuelson, from *Newsweek,* April 8, 1996. Copyright © 1996, Washington Post Writers Group. Reprinted with permission.

Excerpts reprinted by permission from *Cultural Anthropology: An Applied Perspective,* Second Edition, by Gary Ferraro. Copyright © 1995 by West Publishing Company. All rights reserved.

Excerpt from "The American Family: There Is No Normal" in *Life Magazine,* June 1, 1992.

Excerpt from *Cultural Anthropology: A Perspective on the Human Condition* (3rd ed.) by Emily A. Schultz and Robert H. Lavenda, Mayfield Publishing Company, 1995.

Excerpt from Dr. Nancy Levine, "Kinship," a lecture from Anthropology 9: Cultural Anthropology, at the University of California, Los Angeles, March 1, 1996.

"Romantic Love" from *Sociology: The Core,* Second Edition, by James W. Vander Zanden. Copyright © 1990, 1986 by McGraw Hill. Reprinted by permission of the McGraw Hill Companies.

Excerpt from *The Bird Artist* by Howard Norman. Copyright © 1994 by Howard Norman. Reprinted by permission of Farrar, Straus and Giroux, Inc.

Excerpt from "Family Statuses and Roles" in *Society: A Brief Introduction* by Ian Robertson, Worth Publishers, New York, 1989. Reprinted with permission.

Photo Credits

pages 1–2: Four photos by Donna Brinton.

page 18: American quilt photo courtesy of the Pelham Quilters, Pelham, NY.

page 27: Four photos by Donna Brinton.

page 29: Photo by Herlinde Koelbl in *Das Deutsche Wohnzimmer,* published by List. Copyright © 1995 by Herlinde Koelbl.

page 30: Photo by Herlinde Koelbl courtesy of Stock Boston.

page 41: From *My Room: Teenagers in Their Bedroom*s by Adrienne Salinger. Copyright © 1995. Published by Chronicle Books, San Francisco.

page 42: TV and car interior photos from *Red White Blue and God Bless You: A Portrait of Northern New Mexico* by Alex Harris. Copyright © 1992 by Alex Harris. Courtesy of the University of New Mexico Press.

page 61: Photo by Donna Brinton.

page 142: Interracial family photo by Gale Zucker courtesy of Stock Boston; Linda Jensen family photo by Donna Brinton.

Art Credits

page 14: Gravemarkers from "Folk Objects" by Simon J. Bronner, in *Folk Groups and Folklore Genres: An Introduction,* Elliott Oring, ed. Copyright © 1986 by Utah State University Press. Reprinted by permission. All rights reserved.

page 45: Illustration by Milo Winter in *The Aesop for Children,* Rand McNally & Co.,1919.

pages 60, 64, 74, 79: Illustrations from *Essentials of Meteorology: An Introduction to the Atmosphere* by C. Donald Ahrens. Reprinted by permission. Copyright © 1993 by West Publishing Company. All rights reserved.

page 78: Cartoon "Calvin and Hobbes" by Bill Watterson. Used by permission of Universal Press Syndicate.

page 94: Jacob Lawrence, *The Migration of the Negro, Panel No. 3,* 1940–41. Copyright © The Phillips Collection, Washington, D.C.

page 126: Statue of Liberty by Duane Gillogly.

page 169: Cartoon "The Dish and the Spoon." Copyright © 1995 by John O'Brien, from The Cartoon Bank™, Inc.